ONCE AGAIN IN PUBLIC EDITION

The Witches' Almanac

SPRING 1996 —SPRING 1997

For the first time combining the mysterious wiccan and arcane
secrets of an old England witch with one from New England

D0897236

Prepared and edited by
ELIZABETH PEPPER and JOHN WILCOCK

CONTAINING pictorial and explicit delineations of the magical phases of
the Moon together with full and complete information about astrological
portents of the year to come and various aspects of occult knowledge
enabling all who read to improve their lives in the old manner.

The Witches' Almanac, Ltd.
Newport
in cooperation with
Capra Press, Santa Barbara

Address all inquiries and information to
THE WITCHES' ALMANAC, LTD.
P.O. Box 4067
Middletown, Rhode Island 02842

ISBN: 0-88496-407-8

First Printing January 1996

Printed in the United States of America

Preface

How often has magic touched your life? The joy of falling in love, the warmth of family harmony, or the comfort of a friend's sympathy are treasured moments. And then there's the reality of one starry night, or a walk in a pine forest, or the sight of ocean waves surging toward the shore that leave us breathless and in awe. Some magical moments are apt to catch us by surprise, like a sneeze — perhaps a concert when we hear a haunting melody, a painting in a museum that seems to speak directly to us, a book or theater performance that leaves us thrilled. The artist created this magic and the world is richer for it.

Dancer / choreographer Martha Graham, for instance, inspired creativity by her work and her words. In *Dance to the Piper*, by colleague Agnes De Mille, Graham stated:

"There is a vitality, a life-force, an energy, a quickening that is translated through you into action and because there is only one of you in all of time, this expression is unique. And if you block it, it will never exist through any other medium and be lost. The world will not have it. It is not your business to determine how good it is nor how valuable nor how it compares with other expressions. It is your business to keep it yours clearly and directly."

Later, in her published *Notebooks*, Graham with a flash of insight remarked, "I suddenly knew what witchcraft is — in microcosm. It is the being within each of us — of creative energy, no matter in what area or direction of activity."

HOLIDAYS

Spring 1996 to Spring 1997

CONTENTS

ELIZABETH PEPPER & JOHN WILCOCK
Executive Editors

JEAN MARIE WALSH
Associate Editor

Astrologer	Dikki-Jo Mullen
Climatologist	Tom C. Lang
Flora and Fauna	Kerry Cudmore
Contributing Editor	Barbara Stacy
Production	Bendigo Associates
Circulation	Bill McCarthy
Sales & Marketing	Kevin Murphy

ODE

We are the music-makers,
  And we are the dreamers of dreams,
Wandering by lone sea-breakers,
  And sitting by desolate streams;
World-losers and world-forsakers,
  On whom the pale moon gleams:
Yet we are the movers and shakers
  Of the world for ever, it seems.

—ARTHUR O'SHAUGHNESSY
1844 - 1881

today and tomorrow

By Oliver Johnson

APOCALYPSE SOON?: The impending millenium has perhaps unsurprisingly raised the anxiety level of those who believe that the figure 2000 possesses extraordinary significance; and Ted Daniels, a folklore scholar, is busier than he's ever been. Daniels, 57, produces a monthly newsletter, *Millenial Prophecy Report*, which tracks the hundreds of groups that think the apocalypse is at hand. "It's like when the odometer ticks over in your car, but on a global scale," he says, referring to what some think will be Doomsday. Prophecies, prognostications, and dire predictions pour into Daniels' Philadelphia office by the sackload. An unusually large percentage of them are from Sedona, Arizona which he describes as "the Vatican City of the New Age movement." Strangely enough, the missives are mostly optimistic; focusing on prophecies "in which some sort of divine or cosmic power wipes out world evil and ushers in an era of peace and beauty," as one writer put it. Most of these seem based upon the fairly common belief

that life began as a sort of paradise and, although it took a wrong turn somewhere, will eventually find its way back. When it comes to forecasting what's going to happen in the year 2000, it seems as if everybody has a theory—UFO groups, psychics, radio evangelists, Christian ministries, even geologists. "The millenium," says Daniels, "is a hot property."

AZTEC REMEDIES: South of the border, the spiralling cost of manufactured medicines is causing a boom in pre-Colombian remedies, many of which—especially in rural areas—are still known by their indigenous names, reports *Mexico Now* . Revealing that about 25 percent of today's prescription drugs were discovered as natural plant compounds (most of them modified versions of folk remedies), the bimonthly newsletter said that the Aztecs' pharmaceutical knowledge has been preserved by rural *curanderos* and "has often served as the basis for spectacular modern-day scientific discoveries." Entire sections of every big city or village market are piled high with fragrant grasses, leaves, barks,

flowers, seeds, and roots, the writer added. Among those which can usually be found are *arnica*, which is used as a poultice for wounds and bruises; *aloe vera* for skin disorders; *tomillo* (thyme) for digestion; *berro* (watercress) applied to the temples to relieve headaches; *albahaca* (basil) inhaled to clear sinuses; and *litsea glaucescens* (Mexican laurel) for sore throats.

NATURAL REMEDIES: Meanwhile, the National Cancer Institute announced that it is testing as many as 20,000 extracts of natural products every year to supplement such successful drugs as *vincristine* from Madagascar's rosy periwinkle plant and *taxol* derived from the Pacific yew tree. Gordon Cragg, chief of the NCI's natural products division, says 99.5% of the world's plants have yet to be investigated for their medical value. "Nature is still in many cases the most economical source for medicines," he says.

LOTSA LUCK: Sometime this year England's University of Hertfordshire will be collating the results of its two-year study of the psychology of luck which it hopes will explain why some people are more favored by good fortune than others. One of the things that may be decided is whether "lucky"

people are simply those who selectively remember only the good things that happen to them. Richard Wiseman, 30, a senior lecturer who is conducting the research, explains: "If someone believes they are lucky to start with, they are more likely to persist in the face of failure. Unlucky people do the opposite: they don't buy lottery tickets because they 'know' they won't win so it becomes a self-fulfilling prophecy." Those taking part in the survey first had to fill out a questionnaire estimating what they believed to be their own luck quotient, which was then tested against such random events as how often they could correctly predict the toss of a coin or guessing the shape of a drawing hidden inside an envelope.

PERCEPTIVE PETS: After investigating claims from dozens of people that their pets always anticipated their homecoming by stationing themselves in the window or even the driveway, a London biologist maintains that some cats and dogs seem to possess a supernatural "sixth sense." Dr. Rupert Sheldrake's research into perceptive pets was persuasive enough to earn a grant from New York's Lifebridge Foundation which is financing controlled experiments. In the first of these, an Austrian television crew followed a

Lancashire woman around her village while a second unit remained at her home filming her dog—which padded to the window to sit and wait at the exact moment she began her return. There had been no contact between the two groups, but the times were a perfect match. Commenting on this and the innumerable examples he had been given of similar behavior (including a cat that bounded to the telephone only when his mistress called), Dr. Sheldrake says, "These observations are very intriguing. They appear to show that there does exist an invisible bond between pets and their owners which may go beyond known forces."

PIGEON POWER: Until last year there were still 5,000 pigeons working for the Swiss regular army, but now—just before Switzerland hosts the International Racing Pigeon Olympiad in 1997—they have been demobilized, bringing to an end 2,000 years of military flying. Most of the pigeons will be taken care of by private fanciers.

"It's a great irony that this should happen now," says Rick Osman, editor of *Racing Pigeon Weekly*. "We had hoped to celebrate the Swiss army pigeon service at the Olympiad." The magazine was founded by Rick's great-grandfather who ran the World War I

pigeon loft in London; his son, in turn, ran the World War II pigeon service, carrying messages almost as swiftly and much more safely than radio waves which proved easier to intercept. The French even experimented with sending "photographer pigeons" high above the enemy trenches with miniature cameras strapped to their chests. Pigeons relayed the news of Caesar's conquest of Gaul to a waiting Roman world and flew a regular communications service for Genghis Khan between Europe and Asia. Osman believes they could be even more valuable today as a sort of feathered Federal Express. "Microchip technology means a single pigeon can carry 200 pages of information on 10 chips," he explains, "with four chips carried on the leg capsule and a further six in a neck container."

FROM NEAR & FAR: Drivers born under the sign of Aries are the most likely to have accidents, with Pisces and Virgo in second and third place, according to an insurance company, Zurich Municipal, whose tables show Sagittarians as having the least accidents....A couple who spent almost $700,000 on an allegedly haunted 13th-century house in Lancashire intending to turn it into a tourist attraction are suing the vendors for misrepresentation after finding no ghosts....James Gibson, a California planetary scientist who named an asteroid after his cat Mr. Spock, has raised the ire of astronomers who think the name is undignified. About a quarter of the 6,057 known asteroids are registered at the Minor Planetary Center in Cambridge, Massachusetts.

The Tarot Key of Strength

The Enchantress. The Charmer. The Witch. Once known as Lady of the Beasts, Goddess of the Cosmic Lion, the Queen of the Animals she stands between or sits enthroned upon lions. She dominates the creatures of the animal world but does not fight them; between them there is no hostility or antagonism. She rules over the unconscious powers that take animal form in our dreams. She handles that which

Tarot de Marseille   Nicolas Conver, 1761

prowls and howls just outside the safe walls of culture and consciousness.

Strength knows that all the impulse and anxiety of the individual and the community must ultimately be subordinated to the life and purpose of the species. It is the spiritual order of the whole that appears as the Lady of the Beasts. She is the strength and vitality of the life force that manifests through the feminine, whose ultimate purpose is the continuation of the species, who represents love without division, love without judgment. She is the power of love to tame the inhuman forces of life through her gentle touch and the direct physical contact of human relationships.

She is the heroine of Beauty and the Beast, the Princess and the Frog Prince, she is the love that delivers man from his beastly role. Through woman's compassion a hideous monster can reveal itself as lover, god, or savior.

She is Leda and Europa; humanity penetrated by a god-force that desires to move through her. She is Demeter of the Lions or Cybele, described in ancient texts as "the Virgin in her heavenly place (who) rides upon the Lion." She is Medusa, the Gorgon, who uses the strength of lions to aid and assist

10

her in her role as midwife. She is Psyche whose impossible tasks can only be performed by instinct.

She is the Loathly Lady of a myth in which a handsome knight, in order to save the life of King Arthur, must answer the question, "What does woman want?" A hideous old woman gives him the answer in return for his marrying her. To his dismay he must choose if she is to be beautiful in the day and ugly at night or vice versa. Upon leaving the decision to the lady, the spell is broken, for the answer to "What does woman want?" is to "have her own sovereignty," that is her own choice.

Yet centuries later we still battle the question of whether woman has the right to choose what will happen to her own body. If the wise message of the myth is heeded, the answer will be yes. Meanwhile, witchcraft and enchantment remain the only means of protection for women and those they love. The Hermetic Order of the Golden Dawn taught that the dark persona (or shadow), could become a strong yet trained animal — "a mighty steed, a powerful beast" — on which a person could ride, giving greatly added strength. This Tarot card represents the feminine tempering the force of Nature with love and compassion, embracing it with understanding and thus giving it a place in the world so that civilization can emerge.

Strength gives us fortitude, the energy for work and creativity, the desire to exert ourselves with a force beyond the reach of the conscious mind. Strength is our basic survival mechanism, whether as anger and rage rebelling against whatever threatens life, or as lust leading to the regeneration of the species or the expression of our own creativity. The strongest power in the world is love. Just as we can conquer all through love, we must learn to love all parts of our nature — the bestial and the divine.

—MARY K. GREER

Author of the classic *Tarot for Your Self*, Greer's latest work is *Women of the Golden Dawn*.

Rider Deck   Pamela Colman Smith, 1910

RUMPELSTILTSKIN

Illustrations by Margaret Evans Price, 1921.

THERE was once upon a time a poor miller who had a beautiful daughter. Now it happened one day that he had an audience with the King, and in order to make himself seem important, he said, "I have a daughter who can spin straw into gold."

The King said to the miller, "That's an art that interests me. If your daughter is as skilled as you say, bring her to my castle tomorrow, and I'll put her to the test."

When the girl was brought to him, the King conducted her to a chamber full of straw, gave her a spinning wheel and spindle, and said, "Now set to work. You have the night, and if by tomorrow at dawn you have not spun this straw into gold, you must die." With that, he locked the door of the chamber, and left her alone inside.

There sat the poor miller's daughter, and didn't know what in the world she was to do. She had not the least idea how to spin straw into gold, and she became more and more distressed until at last she began to weep. Then all at once the door sprang open, and in stepped a little man who said, "Good evening, miller's daughter, why are you crying so hard?" "Oh," answered the girl, "I'm supposed to spin straw into gold, and I don't know how to do

it." The little man said, "What will you give me if I spin it for you?" "My necklace," said the girl.

The little man took the necklace, sat down before the spinning wheel, and whir, whir, whir, in a trice the bobbin was full. Then he put on another, and whir, whir, whir, the wheel went round three times, and the second was full. And so it went on till morning, when all the straw was spun and all the bobbins were full of gold.

As soon as the sun rose the King came, and when he saw all the gold he was astonished and delighted, but his heart lusted all the more after gold. He had the miller's daughter taken to another room full of straw, much bigger than the first, and bade her to spin that too, in one night, if she valued her life. The girl didn't know what to do, and she was weeping when the door opened as before and the little man appeared and asked, "What will you give me if I spin the straw into gold for you?" "The ring on my finger," answered the girl. The little man took the ring, began to whir again at the wheel, and by dawn he had spun all the straw into glittering gold.

The King was overjoyed at the sight, but his greed for gold was still not satisfied. So he had the miller's daughter taken to an even larger chamber full of straw and said, "You still have to spin all of this tonight; but if you succeed you shall become my wife." "She's only a miller's daughter, it's true," he thought, "but I'd never find a richer woman if I were to search the whole world over."

When the girl was alone the little man came for the third time and

said, "What will you give me if I spin the straw for you this time?" "I've nothing more to give," answered the girl. "Then promise me your first child if you become Queen."

"Who knows what might happen?" thought the miller's daughter, and, besides, she did not see any other way out of her difficulty. She promised the little man what he demanded, and in return he spun the straw into gold once more. When the King came in the morning and found that everything had gone as he desired, he married her, and the miller's beautiful daughter became a Queen.

When a year had passed a fine son was born to her, but the Queen had forgotten all about the little man when he suddenly entered her chamber and said, "Now give me what you promised." The Queen was terrified and offered the little man all the riches of the kingdom if he would let her keep her child. But the little man said, "No, I would rather have a living creature than all the treasures of the world."

13

Then the Queen began to moan and weep to such an extent that the little man was sorry for her. "I will give you three days," said he, "and if within that time you can guess my name you may keep the child."

Now the Queen pondered all night long over all the names she had ever heard, and sent a messenger all over the country to inquire far and wide what other names there were. When the little man arrived the following day, she began with Casper, Melchior, and Balthazar, and all the names she knew, one after another. But after each one, the little man said, "That's not my name." The second day she had inquiries made all round the neighborhood for the names of people living there, and suggested to the little man all the most unusual and strange names — Cowribs, Spindleshanks, Bootlace — but his answer was always: "That's not my name."

On the third day the messenger returned and announced, "I've not found any new names, but as I was passing the corner of a wood near a high hill, where the fox says good night to the hare, I saw a little house, and in the front of the house burned a fire, and round the fire an odd little man was hopping about on one leg and singing:

Tomorrow I brew, today I bake,
And then the child away I'll take;
For little deems my royal dame
That Rumpelstiltskin is my name!

You can imagine the Queen's delight at hearing the name, and when the little man arrived shortly afterwards and asked, "Now, my lady Queen, what is my name?" She asked first: "Is your name Conrad?" "No." "Is your name Hal?" "No." "Is your name, perhaps, Rumpelstiltskin?"

"The fairies told you that, the fairies told you that!" shrieked the little man, and in his rage he stamped his right foot into the ground so hard that it sank up to his waist; then in a passion he seized his left leg with both hands and tore himself in two.

—THE BROTHERS GRIMM, 1812.

The Theatre, from Terence, *Comoediae*   Lyon, 1493.

This whole creation is essentially subjective, and the dream is the theatre where the dreamer is at once scene, actor, prompter, stage manager, author, audience, and critic.

—CARL G. JUNG

MOON GARDENING

BY PHASE

Sow, transplant, bud and graft *Plow, cultivate, weed and reap*

NEW	First Quarter	FULL	Last Quarter	NEW
Plant above-ground crops with outside seeds, flowering annuals.	Plant above-ground crops with inside seeds.		Plant root crops, bulbs, biennials, perennials.	Do not plant.

BY PLACE IN THE ZODIAC

Fruitful Signs

Cancer - Most favorable planting time for all leafy crops bearing fruit above ground. Prune to encourage growth in Cancer.

Scorpio - Second only to Cancer, a Scorpion Moon promises good germination and swift growth. In Scorpio, prune for bud development.

Pisces - Planting in the last of the Watery Triad is especially effective for root growth.

Taurus - The best time to plant root crops is when the Moon is in the sign of the Bull.

Capricorn - The Earthy Goat Moon promotes the growth of rhizomes, bulbs, roots, tubers and stalks. Prune now to strengthen branches.

Libra - Airy Libra may be the least beneficial of the Fruitful Signs, but is excellent for planting flowers and vines.

Barren Signs

Leo - Foremost of the Barren Signs, the Lion Moon is the best time to effectively destroy weeds and pests. Cultivate and till the soil.

Gemini - Harvest in the Airy Twins; gather herbs and roots. Reap when the Moon is in a sign of Air or Fire to assure best storage.

Virgo - Plow, cultivate, and control weeds and pests when the moon is in Virgo.

Sagittarius - Plow and cultivate the soil or harvest under the Archer Moon. Prune now to discourage growth.

Aquarius - This dry sign of Air is perfect for ground cultivation, reaping crops, gathering roots and herbs. It is a good time to destroy weeds and pests.

Aries - Cultivate, weed, and prune to lessen growth. Gather herbs and roots for storage.

Consult our Moon Calendar pages for phase and place in the zodiac circle. The Moon remains in a sign for about two and a half days. Match your gardening activity to the day that follows the Moon's entry into that zodiac sign.

The MOON Calendar

 is divided into zodiac signs rather than the more familiar Gregorian calendar.

1996   1997

 Bear in mind that new projects should be initiated when the Moon is waxing (from dark to full): when the Moon is on the wane (from full to dark), it is a time for storing energy and the wise person waits.

Please note that Moons are listed by day of entry into each sign.Quarters are marked, but as rising and setting times vary from one region to another, it is advisable to check your local newspaper, library or planetarium.

The Moon's Place is computed for Eastern Standard Time

DARKNESS TO LIGHT

As early as 1000 B.C., observers of the sky in China and Babylon recognized patterns of solar and lunar eclipses and devised systems by which to predict their appearances. The knowledge quickly dispersed throughout the ancient world. By classical times, most literate cultures knew precisely when to expect the Sun or the Moon to vanish from sight briefly and then emerge as bright as before. Interpretation of the phenomena varied from culture to culture according to particular situations as well as the governing astrological forces. A total lunar eclipse was generally considered a portent of beneficial change.

Twice during 1996, in April and September, the Earth will cast its shadow across the Full Moon in total lunar eclipse. The Moon will not be obliterated, but will appear instead as a dim disk glowing pale red by light refracted from the Earth's atmosphere. The double eclipses of 1996 are unique, for the Aries Moon falls in the sign of Libra and the Libra Moon in Aries, twice combining the two Cardinal Signs of Fire and Air in total eclipse. This particular astrological configuration has occurred only nine times in this century, most recently on April 12 and October 6 in 1968. The message to the world of witches is clear. Nature presents us with two magical timespans in which to divine that which is hidden.

ARIES ECLIPSE - April 3: *Sun in Aries, Moon in Libra.* The initial phase begins before Moonrise in late afternoon. By the time the Moon appears over the eastern horizon, it will be in partial shadow. Totality, as the Moon passes into the center or deepest part of the Earth's shadow, is from 6:27 P.M. to 7:53 P.M., EST. The eclipse will be visible in the eastern and central United States and Canada.

LIBRA ECLIPSE - September 26: *Sun in Libra, Moon in Aries.* Most of North America will see the darkened Full Moon. The interval of totality is from 10:19 P.M. to 11:29 P.M., EDST; in the west: 7:19 P.M. to 8:29 P.M., PDST. Saturn shines brightly nearby as the shadow of Earth dims the Moon.

A total lunar eclipse is a microcosm of a complete Moon cycle — Full to Dark and back to Full within a space of hours. During the periods of totality — when the elements of Fire and Air symbolically illuminate the Moon's mystic darkness — study the illustration above. Use it as an object for meditation as the Tibetans employ their mandalas. It is said that when you give yourself up to complete and utter concentration, the mind will give you information from a source beyond reason. *So mote it be.*

aries	March 21- April 20

Mars   *Cardinal Sign of Fire*

s	m	τ	w	τ	f	s
			1996 Vernal Equinox	Mar. **21** Taurus	**22** *The wind is green*	**23** Gemini
24 *Measure the odds*	**25**	**26** ◑ Cancer	**27**	**28** *Trust your heart* Leo	**29**	**30** *Walk in the woods*
31 *Christopher Walken born, 1943* Virgo	Apr. **1** *Fools rush in*	**2** *Plan ahead* Libra	**3** ◯ seed moon total lunar eclipse	**4** WANING Scorpio	**5** *Bette Davis born, 1908*	**6** *Go back in time*
7 *Spring one hour ahead* Sagittarius	**8**	**9** *Observe caution* Capricorn	**10** ◑	**11** Aquarius	**12** *Baffle enemy with laughter*	**13** Pisces
14 *Resist negative notion*	**15**	**16** *Seek a hidden path*	**17** ● Partial Solar Eclipse Taurus	**18** WAXING	**19**	**20** *Find the New Moon* Gemini

Europa and the Sacred Bull   Saragossa, 1488.

EUROPA AND THE BULL

While picking flowers with her maidens along the shore, Europa, princess of Sidon, saw a beautiful bull, white as untrodden snow. Timid at first, she presently held out a bunch of flowers and the creature licked her hand. Then she called to her companions: "Come, dear playmates ... let us mount the bull here and take our pastime, for truly, he will bear us on his back, and carry all of us; and how mild he is, and dear, and gentle to behold, and no whit like other bulls!"

She mounted him, but before her companions could follow, the bull leaped up and sped toward the sea. The beautiful beast was Zeus in disguise, who had fallen in love with Europa and had assumed this form to carry her off. He swam to Crete and there Europa became the mother of Minos, the great Cretan king, and of Rhadamanthus, the judge of the dead in the underworld.

—MOSCHUS, *Idyls*, II, 150 B.C.

taurus — April 21- May 21

Venus   *Fixed Sign of Earth*

s	m	т	w	т	ƒ	s
April **21** *Obey a whim*	**22** Cancer	**23** *Shirley Temple born, 1928*	**24**	**25** Leo	**26** *Flee hypocrisy*	**27** *Lighten up* Virgo
28	**29** *Collect sea water* Libra	**30** Beltane Eve	May **1** ROODMAS	**2** *Accept a challenge* Scorpio	**3** hare moon	**4** WANING Sagittarius
5 *Sing before breakfast*	**6** *Willie Mays born, 1931* Capricorn	**7**	**8** White Lotus Day Aquarius	**9** Lemuria	**10** Pisces	**11** *Least said, easiest mended*
12 *Bow to the inevitable* Aries	**13**	**14** *Cast a cold eye*	**15** Taurus	**16** *Revel in freedom*	**17** Gemini	**18** WAXING
19 *Greet the Sunrise* Cancer	**20**	**21** *Abide by the rules*				

The Tea of Tranquillity

Here is a delightful tea blend which you can easily make yourself. It produces a calming, grounding effect.

Mix:
    2 parts Red Clover blossoms
    2 parts Rose Hips
    1 part German Chamomile flowers
    1 part Peppermint leaves

Red Clover - *Trifolium pratense*. Red Clover is found abundantly in fields throughout eastern and central U.S. Gather the flowering tops of this herb when the dew is still on it, then make sure the plant is dried thoroughly before storing. This delightful herb contributes a grounding, purifying influence to this tea blend.

Rose Hips - *Rosa rugosa*. This Asian native can be found along the seasides of northern U.S. and Canada, or may be purchased in herb shops. Rose hips are said to regulate vital energy, contributing a nourishing boost of vitamin C to this blend. Collect the ripe hips when they are red and still firm. It will take weeks of patient drying to ensure safe storage of this fleshy fruit.

German Chamomile - *Matricaria chamomilla*. The flowers of this alien species are gathered just before they open, if you choose to grow your own. Otherwise, this herb is readily available in herb shops. Chamomile adds a relaxing, soothing note to this mixture.

Peppermint - *Mentha piperita*. Often found as an escaped cultivar in wet areas throughout eastern and central U.S., peppermint is a delightful, easy-to-grow companion in any garden. Harvest the leaves before flowers begin to develop, drying thoroughly before storing. Peppermint blends and activates other herbs within formulas, and will also help calm "nervous stomachs."

—KERRY CUDMORE

Ⅱ	**gemini**	**May 22- June 21**
	Mercury	*Mutable Sign of Air*

s	*m*	*т*	*w*	*т*	*F*	*s*
			May **22** *Avoid danger* Leo	**23**	**24** *Queen Victoria born, 1819*	**25** Virgo
26 *Stay grounded* Capricorn	**27** Libra	**28** *Wear a mask*	**29** Oak Apple Day Scorpio	**30** *Consult a candle flame*	**31** *Achieve a victory* Sagittarius	June **1** dyad moon
2 WANING Capricorn	**3** *Cast away a burden*	**4** Night of the Watchers Aquarius	**5** *Forget regret*	**6** Pisces	**7** *Paul Gaugan born, 1848*	**8**
9 *Keep wits about you* Aries	**10**	**11** Taurus	**12** *View life from a hilltop*	**13** Gemini	**14** *Advance with hope*	**15**
16 WAXING Cancer	**17** *Weave a spell*	**18** Leo	**19** *Spirits are high*	**20** Midsummer Night	**21** SUMMER SOLSTICE Virgo	

The Moon and the Weather

Pale Moon doth rain,
Red Moon doth blow,
White Moon doth neither
Rain nor snow.

Clear Moon, frost soon.

A dark mist over the Moon
is a promise of rain.

The heaviest rains fall
following the New and the
Full Moons.

The Full Moon eats the
clouds away.

A New Moon and a windy night
Sweep the cobwebs out of sight.

A Red Moon is a sure sign of
high winds.

And should the Moon wear a halo
of red, a tempest is nigh.

Many rings around the Moon
signal a series of severe
blasts.

A single ring around the
Moon that quickly vanishes
heralds fine weather.

When the New Moon holds
the Old Moon in its arms
(ring around the New Moon)
disasters at sea occur.

Sharp horns on the Sickle
Moon indicate strong winds.

When the moon's horns point up,
the weather will be dry.

When the Moon's horns point
down, rain spills forth.

Blunt horns on a Crescent
Moon presage a long spell
of fair weather.

cancer June 22- July 23

Moon   *Cardinal Sign of Water*

s	m	т	w	т	f	s
						June **22** *Forgive an injury*
23 Eve of St. John Libra	**24** St.John's Day	**25**	**26** *Gather wild herbs* Scorpio	**27**	**28** *Lena Horne born, 1917* Sagittarius	**29** *Draw down the Blue Moon*
30 mead moon Capricorn	July **1** WANING	**2** *Venus smiles* Aquarius	**3** *Seek a message in the clouds*	**4** Pisces	**5** *Judge not*	**6** *Open your heart* Aries
7	**8** Taurus	**9** *The wind is red*	**10**	**11** *Rejoice in being* Gemini	**12**	**13** *Spend time alone* Cancer
14 *Woody Guthrie born, 1912*	**15**	**16** WAXING Leo	**17** *Determine your course*	**18** Virgo	**19** *Leave offering at the well*	**20** *Wish on the Moon*
21 *Keep your word* Libra	**22**	**23** Scorpio				

ANIMAL TIPS

When handling sheep or goats, resist the temptation to grab onto their horns. They will strongly and furiously panic if held in this manner.

Man's fascination with the pigeon (family *Columbidae*) dates back to 3000 B.C. Pigeons, being as abundant as they are around human dwellings, are an easy bird to watch. The habits of pigeons are very alike around the world. All are monogamous and are attentive to their mates. Both sexes assist in constructing their frail nest, which usually accomodates two eggs. The female attends the nest at night, while the male takes over during daylight hours. The young, which are hatched with their eyes sealed, remain in the nest for 12 to 18 days. The pigeons' favorite foods are seeds, fruit, berries and some insects, but they are wonderfully adaptive garbage collectors in cities and suburban areas.

When introducing a new cat or dog to other animals in your home, keep your interference to a cautious minimum. The aggressive posturings, growlings, and hissings will rarely escalate beyond mere body language. These activities may seem threatening, but are very necessary to the reconstruction of social hierarchies within the home.

If your house tends to be dry during the winter, causing your canine companions to suffer from dry, itchy skin, you may take the following steps. Add 1 tablespoon brewer's yeast per 50 pounds of body weight to each feeding. Mix this with a small amount of any nut or seed oil into the food. This will help nourish the skin. Bathing is also recommended to provide a quick relief to the itchy dander which accumulates when the coat is dry.

When handling horses it is standard to always begin from the horses' left side. All grooming procedures are started from the left side, and leading and mounting are also done on this side. This is a very convenient safe-guard against unexpectedly spooking your equine companion.

Goats are not grazing animals, but have more of a browsing nature. Goats require a portion of twigs, branches, and the bark of woodland trees along with their staple diet. An easy way to provide this is to drive goats into a wooded area for daily foraging. Goats are herd-conscious animals, and are easily driven in groups.

—KERRY CUDMORE

Pierre Bonnard, c. 1906.

26

♌ leo	July 24- August 23					

Sun   *Fixed Sign of Fire*

s	**m**	**τ**	**w**	**τ**	**F**	**s**
			Jul. **24** *Reveal nothing*	**25** Sagittarius	**26** *Laugh and be well*	**27** *Speak your mind* Capricorn
28 *Prepare to reap*	**29** Aquarius	**30** wort moon	**31** WANING Lughnassad Eve Pisces	Aug. **1** LAMMAS	**2** *Myrna Loy born, 1905* Aries	**3** *Allow for change*
4 *Drift for a while* Taurus	**5**	**6**	**7** Gemini	**8** *Strength is a virtue*	**9** Cancer	**10** *Seize the day*
11	**12** *Wear or carry silver* Leo	**13** Diana's Day	**14** Virgo	**15** WAXING	**16** *Dismiss cares*	**17** *Robert DeNiro born, 1943* Libra
18 *Trust your instinct*	**19** Scorpio	**20** *Practice sorcery*	**21** Sagittarius	**22**	**23** *Bless the beasts*	

27

The Fox and the Grapes

A famished fox saw some clusters of ripe black grapes hanging from a trellised vine. She resorted to all her tricks to get at them, but wearied herself in vain, for she could not reach them. At last she turned away beguiling herself of her disappointment and saying: "The grapes are sour, and not ripe as I thought."

MORAL: People who can't get something they were after decide that they don't really want it.

From AESOP'S FABLES. Literally translated from the Greek by George Fyler Townsend, Belford, Clarke & Co., Chicago, 1882.

	virgo	August 24–September 23				
	Mercury		*Mutable Sign of Earth*			

s	*m*	*τ*	*w*	*τ*	*ƒ*	*s*
						Aug. 24 *Take no chances* Capricorn
25 *Maintain your poise*	**26** Aquarius	**27** *Hope and work*	**28** barley moon Pisces	**29** WANING Day of Thoth	**30** Aries	**31** *Think thrice*
Sept. 1 *Gather fallen feathers* Taurus	**2**	**3** *Return a favor* Gemini	**4**	**5** *Louis XIV born, 1638* Cancer	**6** *Patience rewarded*	**7** *Evil is ignorance*
8 *Patsy Cline born, 1932* Leo	**9** *Wear an amulet*	**10** *Guard privacy*	**11** Virgo	**12**	**13** WAXING Libra	**14** *Face the unknown*
15 *Plan a quest* Scorpio	**16**	**17** *Fly by night*	**18** Sagittarius	**19** *As above, so below*	**20** Capricorn	**21** *Find perfect balance*
22 Autumnal Equinox Aquarius	**23** *The lost is found*					

29

 **Medieval Astrology**

One of the most magical and intriguing eras in astrology's long history is linked to the Middle Ages and Renaissance. Spanning the years from about 1100 through 1680, this time period has left us a rich legacy of art and literature with astrological themes which still enchant us today. The portents and wisdom of the stars were respected by everyone and were an integral part of daily life.

A glance at Chaucer's *Canterbury Tales* finds The Wife of Bath referring to her horoscope to indicate the Sun in Taurus, while the Ram and Aries reveal the timing for the departure of the pilgrims to be in early spring. Shakespeare makes use of numerous astrological references; especially in *King Lear, Julius Caesar*, and *Romeo and Juliet*. In 1409 *Les Tres Riches Heures du Duc de Berry* was begun. It is an illumined seasonal calendar showing how the Sun signs guided activities in daily life. The Chartres cathedral in France has a zodiacal wheel stained-glass window that is breathtaking in its beauty and detail. When the sun shines through it, visitors see the twelve signs illuminated in celestial splendor.

The Virgin Queen, Elizabeth I (a Virgo), was a devotee of the stars. The brilliant Dr. John Dee was her court astrologer. His predictions and skillful use of astrology were credited with enhancing the memorable Elizabethan era.

Life was often short and treacherous during the Middle Ages. The astrology of the times reflects that fact.

Contemporary astrologers tend to be positive and humanistic in interpreting the celestial bodies. Not so in earlier times. The horoscope was used as a tool to prescribe herbal medicines or to issue dire warnings.

Below is a list of the luminaries (Sun and Moon) and visible planets used by the medieval astrologer along with their applications.

Sun: Royalty, rank, title, fathers, masculine energy, heat, drought, giver of life.

Moon: Witchcraft, wortcunning, folk magic, sailors, mother, commoners, rainfall, fruitfulness, fertility.

Mercury: Duality, falsehoods, tricksters, scribes and storytellers, travelers, small animals, gardens.

Venus: Jewels, amusements, bards and poets, romance, chivalric love, dances.

Mars: Wars, accidents, fires, dragons and dangerous wild animals, swords and armor, hunting, jousts, tournaments, duels.

Jupiter: The Church, law, pilgrimages, crusades, treasure, convents, monasteries, science, scholarship.

Saturn: Sorrows, death, dungeons, enemies, outlaws, darkness, secrecy, losses.

—DIKKI-JO MULLEN

♎ libra **September 24- October 23** Venus *Cardinal Sign of Air*						

s	*m*	*τ*	*w*	*τ*	*f*	*s*
		Sept **24** *Be discreet* Pisces	**25** Total lunar eclipse ☞	**26** blood moon Aries	**27** WANING	**28** *Travel not this day* Taurus
29 *Force fails*	**30** Gemini	Oct. **1** *Consider the source*	**2** *Richard III born, 1452*	**3** *Play a different tune* Cancer	**4** ◗	**5** *Greed digs a grave* Leo
6	**7** *Hasten slowly*	**8** *Whistle up the wind* Virgo	**9**	**10** *Slay a dragon* Libra	**11**	**12** partial solar eclipse
13 WAXING Scorpio	**14** *Onward and upward*	**15** Sagittarius	**16** Gallus Day	**17** *Please yourself* Capricorn	**18**	**19** ◖ Aquarius
20 *Habits are chains*	**21** *Ursula LeGuin born, 1929* Pisces	**22**	**23** *Proceed with caution*			

31

Homage to Hecate

Hecate never assumed rank in the hierarchy of Mt. Olympus, that Who's Who of the greater Greek pantheon. Yet although considered a minor divinity, she is the most powerful of all deities in the realm of the supernatural. Hecate is the superlative seer, the goddess of sorcery and witchcraft.

The chief symbol of Hecate, oddly enough, is the crossroads, and her name means "she who works from afar." In general and for obvious reasons, the myth symbology of the ancients dealt with great natural forces or significant human concerns — the Sun, the Moon, thunder, the hunt, growth of crops, love, sex, childbirth, and so on. But here we have a symbol that seems enigmatically abstract, until we consider the implications.

Crossroads are psychically potent sites, for at this point travelers center in the triumvirate of time: the past, the road behind; the present, where they stand; and the future, where the roads ahead vanish into the horizon. Different directions, different destinies. It is Hecate who can see down the road not yet taken. She is often depicted with a flaming torch in each hand, bringing light to darkness and clarifying the unknown.

The Romans knew Hecate as Trivia, Goddess of Three Roads, and her statues dotted crossroads everywhere. Here travelers made offerings of food, invoking the goddess of mystery to send good fortune their way along the journey.

What food did the ancients choose to honor the goddess? One source says eggs and fish; another, fish eggs, or roe; still another, goat cheese and bread. An obscure reference mentions the *trigle*, a red mullet, as the kind of fish frequently sacrificed to Hecate. Keeping all these clues in mind, we've created a modern version of a midnight supper for three to relish and pay tribute to a worthy deity.

Red Caviar and Cream Cheese Frittata

3 large eggs
3 teaspoons cold water
2 tablespoons butter
1 package cream cheese (3 oz.)
1 small jar red caviar (salmon roe)

A frittata is the Italian version of an omelet. Open-faced, it requires no flipping and folding and is far easier to prepare than the traditional French omelet.

Break the eggs in a bowl, add the water, and beat until light and foamy. Melt the butter in a seasoned heavy skillet and when it sizzles, quickly pour in the eggs. Cook over low heat until the eggs start to set. Immediately begin to loosen the edges with a fork and tilt the pan to let the uncooked top flow underneath. Shake the pan gently to prevent sticking. This should take about 5 minutes. Dot the top with dollops of cream cheese and scatter the roe over all. Slip under a heated broiler for no more than a minute. Cut the frittata in three wedges and serve from the skillet with a loaf of crusty bread.

scorpio — October 24-November 22

Pluto   *Fixed Sign of Water*

s	m	τ	w	τ	F	s
				Oct. **24** *Refuse all favors* Aries	**25**	**26** (snow moon) Taurus
27 WANING *Daylight Saving Ends 2 AM*	**28** Gemini	**29** *Bela Lugosi born, 1884*	**30** *Wait till the tide turns* Cancer	**31** Samhain Eve	Nov. **1** HALLOW-MAS	**2** *Marie Antoinette born, 1755* Leo
3 (first quarter)	**4** Virgo	**5** *A brown wind sighs*	**6** *Bide your time*	**7** *Gather fallen leaves* Libra	**8**	**9** *Nurture your love* Scorpio
10 (new moon)	**11** WAXING Sagittarius	**12**	**13** *Rest on your laurels* Capricorn	**14**	**15** *Laugh, witch*	**16** HECATE NIGHT Aquarius
17 (last quarter) Pisces	**18**	**19** *Avoid intrigue*	**20** Aries	**21** *Treasure the moments*	**22** *Enjoy peace* Taurus	

The Wonder of Hope

Confidence of a happy outcome often makes the difference between success and failure, even life and death, for hope is at the heart of every endeavor whether it is climbing a mountain, surviving a siege, or winning a game. With a realistic goal in mind, you may add ability, discipline, hard work, sacrifice, time, experience to the mix — and season with good luck. But without hope, you're defeated before you begin. And hope is as mysterious and elusive in quality as our sleeping visions, our dreams.

True hope is swift and flies with
  swallow's wings; Kings it makes
  Gods, and meaner creatures kings.

—SHAKESPEARE

Hope is a waking dream.

—ARISTOTLE

Nothing is hopeless,
  we must hope for everything.

—EURIPIDES

It is certainly wrong to despair;
  and if despair is wrong hope is
  right.

—SIR JOHN LUBBOCK

Whatever enlarges hope
  will also exalt courage.

—SAMUEL JOHNSON

Hope is the last gift given to man,
  and the only gift not given to youth.
  The power of hoping through
  everything, the knowledge that
  the soul survives its adventures,
  that great inspiration comes
  to the middle-aged.

—G. K. CHESTERTON

Hope springs eternal in
  the human breast: Man never is,
  but always to be blest

—ALEXANDER POPE

We hope vaguely but dread precisely.

—PAUL VALERY

Hope is life and life is hope.

—ADELE SHREVE

sagittarius November 23–December 21

Jupiter   *Mutable Sign of Fire*

s	m	т	w	т	f	s
						Nov. 23 *Visit an oak tree*
24 oak moon Gemini	**25** WANING	**26** *Fulfill a duty*	**27** *Jimi Hendrix born, 1942* Cancer	**28**	**29** *Madeleine L'Engle born, 1918* Leo	**30** *Face the music*
Dec. 1 *Experience teaches*	**2** Virgo	**3**	**4** *Gather resources* Libra	**5** *Assume command*	**6** *Make no demands* Scorpio	**7**
8 *Strive for the best*	**9** Sagittarius	**10**	**11** WAXING Capricorn	**12** *Seek the still point*	**13** *An ill wind blows* Aquarius	**14** *The best is yet to come*
15 *Music heals* Pisces	**16** Eve of Saturnalia	**17** Aries	**18** *Carry an acorn*	**19** *Honor the Sun* Taurus	**20** Eve of Yule	**21** WINTER SOLSTICE

GOAT SONG

Since the dawn of time, the goat has held divine significance in many cultures. The sacred robes of Babylonian priests were made of goatskins. The zodiacal Capricorn with head and body of a goat and a fish's tail, was established as early as the 15th century B.C.; the Sea Goat appears engraved on gems dated to the height of Chaldean rule in Babylon. A cuneiform inscription calls the goat "sacred and exalted," — and at that time this sign was designated as the "Father of Light." Despite the glory the goat enjoyed among the ancients, its present reputation as a symbol of lust and evil is due to the devil-lore devised by medieval churchmen.

Perhaps the goat's character as loathsome and unclean began when the early Hebrews chose it as the animal to carry away the sins of the community in an annual rite of atonement. The hapless scapegoat was driven into the wilderness to perish bearing all the blame for crimes committed by others.

How wildly different is the ancient Greek symbolism regarding the same animal. Associated with the gods Dionysos and Pan, the goat represented the pure, spontaneous joy of being alive. The great god Zeus was nurtured by the she-goat Amalthea. Her name is given to the mythical Horn of Plenty, the cornucopia promising its possessor an abundance of all things desired.

We owe the art of drama to the music and dance celebrations honoring Dionysos. The goat and the god were one — the essence of high spirits and joyful abandon. The chorus and dancers wore goatskins and the rites were performed in an orderly manner until a singer named Thespis broke the rules and began a dispute with the choral leader. His action established dialogue and ever after the religious rituals were plays, for the unexpected is in the very nature of the god himself. Thespian became another word for actor. The highest form of drama, the tragedy, means goat song in Greek.

In northern Europe, the goat was revered for its playful nature, a nature firmly ruled by discipline. The love goddess of Germanic tribes rode a goat to the May Eve revels. She held an apple to her lips, a hound and a hare ran beside her and a raven flew overhead. Thor, the red-headed Norse god of thunder, drove a chariot drawn by two fierce goats. Both god and goddess were in complete control of their animals.

The Greeks warn us that when we deny the wildness in human nature, we court disaster. The message from the North is just as wise: we should acknowledge the wildness, use it to advantage, and learn to temper its force with strength and understanding.

♑ capricorn		December 22- January 20				

Saturn   *Cardinal Sign of Earth*

s	*m*	*τ*	*w*	*τ*	*ℱ*	*s*
Dec. 22 *Walk till weary* Gemini	23	24 *wolf moon* Cancer	25 WANING	26 *Take no extreme measures* Leo	27	28 *Find a safe harbor*
29 *Mary Tyler Moore born, 1937* Virgo	30	31 *Dare to be yourself* Libra	Jan. 1 1997	2	3 *Silence has no pitfalls* Scorpio	4
5 *Leave well enough alone* Sagittarius	6 *Keep the channels open*	7 Capricorn	8	9 Feast of Janus Aquarius	10 WAXING	11 *Love beckons* Pisces
12 *A white wind snows*	13 Aries	14 *Cheer a weary heart*	15 Taurus	16 *Life is a banquet*	17	18 *Need not who needs not thee* Gemini
19 *Prepare sabbat candles*	20 *George Burns born, 1896* Cancer					

THE ROWAN TREE

Daleschamps   Lyons, 1586.

So potent is the flower or berry or wood of the rowan or witchwood or quicken or whicken-tree or mountain ash against the wiles of the elf-folk, that dairymaids use it for cream-stirrers and cowherds for a switch.

—WALTER DE LA MARE

The bright red berries of the mountain ash give this tree its Scottish name "rowan" from the Gaelic *rudha-an*, the red one. An older and more romantic name is *luisliu*, flame or delight of the eye. The scarlet berries also account for its growing high on mountains along with the birch, for birds feast on the berries and drop seeds in crevices at altitudes as high as 3000 feet where the tree springs up and flourishes. Although the most common name for the rowan is mountain ash, it has no botanical relation to the true ash save for a resemblance in its smooth grey bark and graceful ascending branches. Other names for the rowan are whitebeam, quicken and witch-wood, the later possibly derives from the Anglo-Saxon root *wic*, meaning pliable.

Scandinavian myths assign the rowan to Thor, god of thunder. All across northern Europe it was the custom to plant rowan trees near farm buildings to gain the favor of Thor and insure safety for stored crops and animals from storm damage. A necklace of rowan beads enlivened the wearer and twigs were carried as protective charms.

Rowan figures prominently in Scottish folklore as a sure means to counteract evil intent. It was believed that a christened person need only touch a suspected witch with rowan wood in order to break a spell as the poet Allan Ramsay wrote:

Rowan tree and red thread,
Will put witches to their speed.

Yet, a century earlier, in the case of Margaret Barclay, such a charm was damning evidence. Brought to trial for witchcraft in the town of Irvine, Ayrshire, Scotland in 1618, her conviction was assured when a piece of rowan tied with red yarn was found in her possession.

 **aquarius** January 21-February 19

Uranus · Fixed Sign of Air

s	m	t	w	t	f	s
		Jan. **21** *There is world enough and time*	**22**	**23** (storm moon) Leo	**24** WANING	**25** *Observe the clouds* Virgo
26 *Clear the decks*	**27** *Let reason be your guide*	**28** Libra	**29** *W.C. Fields born, 1880*	**30** *Don't make waves* Scorpio	**31** ◐	Feb. **1** Oimelc Eve Sagittarius
2 CANDLE-MAS	**3**	**4** *Discard the useless* Capricorn	**5**	**6** *Visit a sacred place* Aquarius	**7** Chinese Year of the Ox	**8** WAXING Pisces
9 *Mia Farrow born, 1945*	**10** Aries	**11** *Let chance guide you*	**12** Taurus	**13** *Define your limits*	**14** ◑ Gemini	**15** *Don't break stride*
16 Cancer	**17** *Banish all fears*	**18**	**19** *Adventure is in the offing* Leo			

39

EARTH, WIND AND SKY

The ancient Egyptian conception of the world is illustrated above. The goddess of the heavens, her body decorated with stars, spans the sky vault supported by four pillars and the god of air. The earth god is prone below. Egyptian cosmogony differed from that of most other cultures in perceiving the earth as male. The Egyptologist, E.A. Wallis Budge, described the qualities of the deities in *Egyptian Religion* (London, 1899):

SHU, son of Ra and Hathor, was the personification of sunlight, air, and wind. He it was who made his way between the gods Seb and Nut and raised up the latter to form the sky, and this belief is commemorated by the figures of this god in which he is represented as a god raising himself up from the earth with the sun's disk on his shoulders. As a power of nature he typified the light, and, standing on the top of a staircase, he raised up the sky and held it up during each day. To assist him in this work he placed a pillar at each of the cardinal points, and the "supports of Shu" are thus the props of the sky.

SEB was the son of Shu, and the "father of the gods," these being Osiris, Isis, Set, and Nephthys. He was originally the god of the earth, but later he became a god of the dead as representing the earth wherein the deceased was laid. One legend identifies him with the goose, the bird which in later times was sacred to him, and he is often called the "Great Cackler," in allusion to the idea that he made the primeval egg from which the world came into being.

NUT was the wife of Seb and the mother of Osiris, Isis, Set, and Nephthys. Originally she was the personification of the sky, and represented the feminine principle which was active at the creation of the universe. According to the old view, Seb and Nut existed in the primeval watery abyss . . . and later Seb became the earth and Nut the sky. These deities were supposed to unite every evening, and to remain embraced until the morning, when the god Shu separated them, and set the goddess of the sky upon his four pillars until the evening. Nut was, naturally, regarded as the mother of the gods and of all things living.

 **pisces** February 20 - March 20

Neptune — *Mutable Sign of Water*

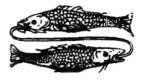

s	m	τ	w	τ	ϝ	s
				Feb. **20** Strengthen your will power	**21** Virgo	**22** (chaste moon)
23 WANING	**24** Libra	**25** George Harrison born, 1943	**26** Scorpio	**27** Discover a mare's nest	**28** Clear your mind	Mar. **1** Matronalia Sagittarius
2	**3** Maintain distance Capricorn	**4**	**5** Help another soul Aquarius	**6**	**7** Kindness pays dividends Pisces	**8** total solar eclipse
9 WAXING Aries	**10** Follow your bliss	**11** Taurus	**12** Dismiss all doubts	**13** Gemini	**14** Life is nature's gift	**15**
16 Look to the future Cancer	**17** The wild birds sing	**18** Leo	**19** Glenn Close born, 1947	**20** Plan a new garden		

A Cycladic Cruise

Three or four times each month, from early spring to late fall, a cruise ship sets sail for the Cyclades, a cluster of Greek isles where the ancient gods are not forgotten. Poseidon, Apollo, Dionysos, Athena—the names beckon all around from the signs on grand hotels and humble tavernas to the insignia of ocean liners and tiny fishing boats.

At Tinos, first stop on this cruise into the past, blue neon letters beside the dock spell out Hotel Poseidona, a modern-day nod to the god whose ruined temple oversees the waves a mile

or two along the coast. Poseidon, second in rank only to Zeus, was undisputed ruler of the sea, rivers, and all underground springs. Poseidon was Lord of Horses, Bull-god, and "earthshaker."Here he was worshipped as "the great doctor," and the island has ever since held a reputation for healing. The 1st-century Roman writer Strabo described the temple as "worthy of a goddess," presumably a reference to Poseidon's wife Amphitrite who shared his honors. Part of an amphora depicting what's believed to be Leto giving birth to Apollo was recovered from the temple and is displayed in the local museum.

Today pilgrims to the island pay tribute to an icon of the Virgin discovered by a now-sainted nun at the site of the hilltop Evangelistra church. This was built atop an earlier temple to Dionysos, partly with stone plundered from the temple of Apollo on Delos.

Speeded by gentle winds, it is south to Delos, the most sacred island of the ancient world, that our ship now heads. Not only the islands encircling Delos but all of Greece is cooled by these Elysian breezes, a gift from Zeus to acknowledge the altar built in his honor in the mountains of Chios by Aristaeus, a son of Apollo.

Once capital of the Delian League, a shipping confederacy, the island was very rich. But power politics ruled then as now and Pericles, the ambitious leader of Athens, looted the Treasury to build the Acropolis which became the League's new headquarters. For hundreds of years before Christ different faiths existed side by side on Delos, the same gods often bearing different names. The statues dedicated to them are arrayed in the local museum, and the barren island is littered with reminders of the zeal with which they were worshipped. Magnificent archways and fallen marble columns all pay a silent tribute to these ancient deities.

Apollo, god of music, symbol of light and reason, was born here on Delos from a wayward encounter between Zeus and Leto. His temple, with scattered fragments of a huge statue, sits close to the sacred (now dry) lake guarded by an elegant row of stone lions of which only five remain. Origi-

nally numbering sixteen, they were installed by Naxos, the island which originally administered the sacred sanctuary before the takeover by Athens. Honored too on Delos—her main temple was at Ephesus—was Artemis, the virgin huntress, who legend credits with assisting at her brother Apollo's birth while herself only nine days old.

In 543 B.C. and again in 420 B.C., Athens "purified" Delos with a decree that nobody could die or be born on the sacred island. And even today sightseers who arrive on the early morning boats from Mykonos are obliged to leave before sundown. A handful of French archaeologists are the only permanent residents.

It is nightfall as our ship noses into the harbor of Naxos, soft lights against the hillside mark the outlines of the little port. Just to the west, an immense, spotlit arch dominates tiny Palatio which is connected by a causeway to the main island. Directly facing Delos, it marks the site of a temple to Apollo begun in 530 B.C. but never completed.

It was to Naxos that Artemis once fled, pursued by Poseidon's twin sons. Changing into a white deer, the virgin goddess lured them to a wooded glade where, hurling javelins at her from opposite sides, they killed each other. Brave Theseus came here too after slaying the monstrous Minotaur in the maze built by Daedalus under the pal-

ace of King Minos in Crete. Exiting the maze with the aid of Ariadne's ball of thread and fleeing with her, Theseus ungallantly abandoned the lady on Naxos' shore and sailed away.

Imprisoned after Theseus' escape, the wily Daedalus sought to evade Minos' patrolling ships and leave Crete by air, constructing wings for himself and his son from feathers and wax. But despite his father's warning, Icarus flew too close to the sun which melted the wax. The Icarian Sea became his tomb.

Meanwhile, back on verdant Naxos, the largest of the Cyclades and supplier of most of its fruit and vegetables, Dionysos once held sway. And it was he who rescued the abandoned Ariadne. Ever licentious, this god of the vine had his own fan club — the Maenads, whom he inspired to ecstatic frenzy. These divine Bacchantes who performed hectic dances expressing "the orgiastic forces of nature" are depicted on vase paintings from as early as the 6th century B.C. Euripides noted in *The Bacchae* that they represented "complete liberation from the conventions of daily life, awakening of primeval instincts, and union with nature."

The ship sails onward. Somewhere in these waters near Mykonos

was the rock to which the sacrilegious Ajax of Locri clung when Poseidon wrecked the ship carrying him home from Troy after the Greeks had sacked the city. The prophet Cassandra, daughter of Troy's King Priam, had warned of the attack but was discredited; when it came, she took refuge in Athena's temple from which she was dragged by Ajax. Furious, Athena demanded that amends be made: "Give the Greeks a bitter homecoming. Stir up the waters with wild whirlwinds when they sail. Let dead men choke the bays and line the shore with wreaths." Poseidon obliged, and with his trident split the rock sheltering the hapless Ajax.

Poseidon's son Triton threw a lump of magic earth into the sea to form Thera, now Santorini. Originally, it was called Calliste (the most beautiful) and its earliest settlers were led by Cadmus, a descendant of Oedipus. Hundreds of steps ascend the steep cliffs to Thera, but ancient Thera was higher still. Here, on the slopes of 1,300-foot Mesa Vouno, extensive ruins mark the sites of temples to Apollo, Dionysos, and Hermes, the god of boundaries, guardian of knaves, and patron deity of shepherds. Often used as a messenger and troubleshooter by the other Olympians, he advised Odysseus to protect himself from Circe's spells by adding the herb moly to his drink. A statue of Hermes is preserved on Andros, the island once ruled by Apollo's son Andron.

Circe herself was not above dispensing advice. She told Odysseus to lash himself to the mast of his ship so that the Sirens' seductive songs would not lure him to steer his craft onto the rocks as had happened to so many others. The Sirens, sea demons mentioned in Homer's *Odyssey* as half-women and half-bird, played the lyre or flute as well as crooning their "celestial harmonies." Few who heard them remained immune.

The Sirens were once ubiquitous in these waters, but today they seem to be silent. At any rate, the crew of our ship never seems to have been tempted and our voyage ends as peacefully as it began.

45

El Niño (n.). A warming of the ocean surface off the western coast of South America that occurs every 4 to 12 years when upwelling of cold, nutrient-rich water does not occur. It causes plankton and fish to die and affects weather over much of the Pacific Ocean.

—THE AMERICAN HERITAGE DICTIONARY, Third Edition

Window on the Weather

Understood holistically, the globe's weather can be seen as a harmonic pattern dominated by the jet stream, powerful air flows shaped like long sine waves. These waves course through both hemispheres, with valleys or "troughs" where storms are born and mountains or "ridges" are related to sun and warmth. The waves determine the ebb and flow of the Earth's climate, transporting heat from the tropics to the poles, and polar air from the Arctic to the tropics. But disruptions such as El Niño generate conditions that can disturb the patterns and bring some marked regional changes.

El Niño results from volcanic eruptions below the ocean that bring unusual weather conditions. But the warmth of El Niño is retreating to be replaced by its opposing form, La Niña. Defined by a sudden sea change cooling the western Pacific, La Niña is expected to bring a warming trend to the western United States and unseasonably cold and wet weather to the East. We may anticipate its effect to last through 1997.

There follow detailed predictions month by month and region by region. But you can get an indication of the immediate weather by simply looking out the window and observing cloud formations. We offer typical clouds to watch for each month of the year.

—TOM C. LANG

SPRING

MARCH, 1996—*Cirrus Clouds*. Also known as Mare's Tails, these clouds consist of ice crystals and occur at high altitudes of 35,000 feet or greater. They are the first indicators of stormy weather, and appear as beautiful wisps against a deep blue sky.

An anticipated split in the jet stream produces varying weather conditions with the pattern favoring late winter snows in the West and early spring for parts of the East. Heavy rains will arrive at low latitudes on the Pacific Coast. Travelers should be wary of mudslides along the coastal range of southern California. Farther east, the storm advances to the peaks of Utah and Colorado, bringing heavy snowfalls. From the plains to the Ohio Valley, there will be sunshine and a milder trend. Then a late-season storm will arrive, bringing wet snow from the Appalachians to the eastern Great Lakes. New England will receive rain from this storm for all but the highest peaks in the north. Above-normal rainfall can be expected from the Gulf Coast as far south as Florida.

APRIL, 1996 — *Stratus Clouds*. Low and gray, these clouds prevail in spring on both coasts when chill winds blow onshore. Often only several hundred feet above ground, such formations can last for days.

April is always a volatile, complex time. Retreating cold air, vigorous winds aloft, and returning warmth sometimes make the month seem like all seasons at once. The jet stream, still strong, bends and spins a wheel of vorticity through the Rockies, blanketing the mountains with snow. Tornadoes will ravage west Texas and Oklahoma by the second week. A Noreaster may begin as chill rain in the Northeast, but quickly change to snow, and snow can result even with temperatures above freezing. Freak late-season storms are still likely in southern California, while spring warmth and two severe thunderstorm outbreaks course through Georgia and Florida.

MAY, 1996—*Cumulus*. The building blocks of larger cloud complexes resulting in thunderstorms, *cumulus* formations are identified by their puffy, congested appearance. Variations include *stratocumulus*, *cumulonimbus* and *altocumulus*.

May brings the heart of the tornado season to Oklahoma and Texas. If the expected jet stream's energy is focused in the mountainous West, numerous severe weather outbreaks can be expected for the Great Plains. High altitude winds will split farther east with a continued wet pattern in Florida, while parts of the Ohio Valley and New England will experience a drought. Late-season rains will be slow to ebb on the Pacific Coast.

SUMMER

JUNE, 1996 — *Cumulus mammatus.* These clouds have a rounded appearance, and they originate from the underside of the smooth anvil that forms at the top of mature thunderstorms. Because they are associated with descending cool air, the atmosphere becomes unstable, sometimes presaging tornadoes and hail.

Tornado genesis is initiated through the interaction of violent updrafts and downdrafts contained within thunderstorms. The jet stream's northward retreat focuses wind energy and the threat of tornadoes from the Great Lakes to New England during June. The Carolinas and Georgia remain relatively dry before easterly waves from the tropics bring rain by midsummer. Frost is still possible in western plateaus, while the spring runoff remains sparkling, turning to a summer torrent. Fog lingers in western harbors as large-scale cyclones beat a hasty retreat past British Columbia.

JULY, 1996 — *Cumulonimbus.* Popularly characterized as "thunderclouds," these are actually a combination of many cloud types that as a complex sometimes tower to 50,000 feet or more.

July is the month for thunderstorms nationwide. Storms in the North move swiftly and are obscured by haze. Look to the West for signs of rough weather — thunder is the usual warning call. Southern storms move more slowly and can erupt overhead. The most likely time for thunderstorm genesis is between 3 p.m. and 9 p.m. Campers should be wary. Flash flooding is possible with these storms in mountainous territory.

AUGUST, 1996 — *Nimbostratus.* Billowy, dark and low hanging. These moisture-laden clouds produce rain and snow and are often obscured during storms. Most often present during the mature stage of cyclones.

Hurricane formation extends farther into the Atlantic during August, with the Cape Verde Islands the most likely point of origin by mid month. The building North Atlantic high-pressure ridge brings heat and humidity to the Eastern Seaboard, with three days in a heat wave in excess of 90 degrees F. Thunderstorms move slowly in the South with flash flooding a threat. An occasional tornado spins close to the Great Lakes. The monsoon season brings afternoon rains along the Continental Divide as far north as Glacier National Park in Montana.

AUTUMN

SEPTEMBER, 1996 — *Altocumulus.* Gray, broken *cumulus* clouds at mid altitude that develop at approximately 10,000 feet. These clouds signal warmer weather and are commonly seen with spiral bands that emanate from tropical storms and hurricanes.

September 10th is the most likely time that a hurricane will slam in somewhere in the Atlantic. The second of a three-year maximum of hurricane activity will bring the threat of violent weather to the East. At this time, it's a good idea to check in with the Weather Channel and other media outlets to keep informed about current hurricane activity. Passing summer heat brings quiet weather to the other regions. Santa Ana winds freshen in the West, with fire threat rising. Unusually cold weather pushes east into the northern Rockies with snow in Montana by September 20th.

OCTOBER, 1996 — *Fog.* Fog consists of low-lying *stratus* clouds that have descended to earth, most commonly during spring and summer across the U.S. in valley locations.

Temperature contrasts through the U.S. reach a minimum in the autumn, resulting in few storms and stable weather patterns. Winds are light, and with lengthening nights fog becomes widespread. Long wave patterns favor high pressure in the East, and low pressure in the Rocky Mountain West. This could reduce Santa Ana winds in California. Hurricanes will form late into October in the Atlantic. One may brush the Atlantic coast, another may approach Texas.

NOVEMBER, 1996 — *Cirrostratus.* A thin veil that partially obscures the Sun and Moon. Comprised of ice crystals, these clouds are found on the leading edge of storm systems and portend rain and snow within 12 hours.

While unstable waves are responsible for the generation of intense winter storms capable of producing heavy snow, it is the stable waves that generally bring the record-breaking early snowfalls. But if a record early snow occurs in your town, expect a mild, snow-free winter! Warmth continues in the East, while record early-season cold continues in the West. Frost is late from New England to the Great Lakes, and balmy days linger longer than normal in the South. Early rainfall can be expected in southern California with snow visible in the surrounding mountains of Los Angeles by the 20th.

WINTER

DECEMBER, 1996 — *Virga*. Precipitation emanating from an overcast sky, not yet reaching the ground. *Virga* has a hazy, opaque appearance that begins at the cloud base and ends several thousand feet below that level as the precipitation evaporates. Common during winter, when air masses preceding storms are dry.

With high pressure dominating the East, the threat of ice storms runs high this December, especially in the valleys of New England, Pennsylvania and North Carolina. The West will be unusually stormy with early-season snows heavy in Denver and the rest of the western Great Plains. Wet weather is also common along the Gulf Coast, with rainfall particularly heavy in Florida, southern Mississippi, Alabama and Georgia.

JANUARY, 1997 — *Arctic Sea Smoke*. Wisps of condensation created by arctic air passing over warm water.

Arctic air is scarce in the East this January and storms are weak and rainy. Fog will be common near the coast, the snowpack slow to form in the mountains. Fierce early winter storms will be common in the West with a split jet stream bringing deep snows to southern California, northern Arizona and southwest Colorado. Residents of Seattle will see snow in the eastern foothills by mid month.

FEBRUARY, 1997 — *Sundog*. This is a phenomenon creating a prism effect as the sun's rays pass through the ice crystals within *cirrus* or *cirrostratus* clouds.

Stormy weather reaches a peak in the West with mudslides a significant threat in California. Early-season tornadoes lash the Gulf Coast and slide further east. Much of the Atlantic Coast and Ohio Valley remain mild with only northern New England experiencing normal winter conditions. Snowfall is particularly heavy in the northern Rockies.

1996 — A LEAP YEAR

A year's date divisible by 4 excepting those divisible by 100 but not by 400 is a leap year of 366 days. Medieval custom became law in Scotland, France, and Italy giving a woman the right to propose marriage to the man of her choice in a leap year, and, if not accepted, to claim from him a silken gown. The next leap year is 2000.

Thirty days hath September,
April, June and November;
All the rest have thirty-one,
Excepting February alone,
And that has twenty-eight days clear
And twenty-nine in each leap year.

presage

by Dikki-Jo Mullen

ARIES 1996 — PISCES 1997

The world changes and we are each transformed.
Exploring the new paths and different places will
bring you to your own unique riches.

The Sun Sign is the familiar zodiac sign we all know as our own. It describes the ego and sense of identity; it shows where we shine. As Earth makes her yearly journey around the Sun, she remains in each sign for about thirty days. The Sun Sign is the best place to start to understand your birth chart's message. It helps you to get a feeling about celestial energies and how they affect you. If you know your Moon Sign and ascendant, check those forecasts for added depth and detail.

If you were born on the day the Sun changes signs, for example, December 21, you are a cusp personality and will combine the qualities of two signs. Your birth year, time, and place indicate which birth sign is actually yours, but you will relate to both forecasts.

Please see Astrological Keys on the next page. The definitions of the planets, signs, houses, and aspects will help you harmonize with your cosmic cycles and guide you through a successful year.

ASTROLOGICAL KEYS

Signs of the Zodiac
Channels of Expression

ARIES: pioneer, leader, competitor
TAURUS: earthy, stable, practical
GEMINI: dual, lively, versatile
CANCER: protective, traditional
LEO: dramatic, flamboyant, warm
VIRGO: conscientious, analytical
LIBRA: refined, fair, sociable
SCORPIO: intense, secretive, ambitious
SAGITTARIUS: friendly, expansive
CAPRICORN: cautious, materialistic
AQUARIUS: inquisitive, unpredictable
PISCES: responsive, dependent, fanciful

Elements

FIRE: Aries, Leo, Sagittarius
EARTH: Taurus, Virgo, Capricorn
AIR: Gemini, Libra, Aquarius
WATER: Cancer, Scorpio, Pisces

Qualities

CARDINAL	FIXED	MUTABLE
Aries	Taurus	Gemini
Cancer	Leo	Virgo
Libra	Scorpio	Sagittarius
Capricorn	Aquarius	Pisces

CARDINAL signs mark the beginning of each new season — active.
FIXED signs represent the season at its height — steadfast.
MUTABLE signs herald a change of season — variable.

Celestial Bodies
Generating Energy of the Cosmos

Sun: birth sign, ego, identity
Moon: emotions, memories, personality
Mercury: communication, intellect, skills
Venus: love, pleasures, the fine arts
Mars: energy, challenges, sports
Jupiter: expansion, religion, happiness
Saturn: responsibility, maturity, realities
Uranus: originality, science, progress
Neptune: dreams, illusions, inspiration
Pluto: rebirth, renewal, resources

Glossary of Aspects

Conjunction: two planets within the same sign or less than 10 degrees apart, favorable or unfavorable according to the nature of the planets.

Sextile: a pleasant, harmonious aspect occurring when two planets are two signs or 60 degrees apart.

Square: a major negative effect resulting when planets are three signs from one another or 90 degrees apart.

Trine: planets four signs or 120 degrees apart, forming a positive and favorable influence.

Quincunx: a mildly negative aspect produced when planets are five signs or 150 degrees apart.

Opposition: a six sign or 180 degrees separation of planets generating positive or negative forces depending on the planets involved.

The Houses — *Twelve Areas of Life*

1st house: appearance, image, identity
2nd house: money, possessions, tools
3rd house: communications, siblings
4th house: family, domesticity, security
5th house: romance, creativity, children
6th house: daily routine, service, health

7th house: marriage, partnerships, union
8th house: passion, death, rebirth, soul
9th house: travel, philosophy, education
10th house: fame, achievement, mastery
11th house: goals, friends, high hopes
12th house: sacrifice, solitude, privacy

ECLIPSES

Eclipses occur at either a Full or New Moon when the Sun, Moon, and Earth are in exact alignment. They exert a strong magnetic pull on the Earth. Unusual weather, significant news, and surprises of all sorts are likely. Meditations and magical workings assume added power if performed at the time of an eclipse. If your birthday is near an eclipse, prepare for a year of changes and growth.

Aries, 1996 - Pisces, 1997 brings five eclipses:

April 3	Total —Full Moon Lunar in Libra
April 17	Partial —New Moon Solar in Aries
September 26	Total— Full Moon Lunar in Aries
October 12	Partial— New Moon Solar in Libra
March 8, 1997	Total— New Moon Solar in Pisces

RETROGRADE MOTION

This describes a planet that appears to be moving backward through the zodiac signs. The backward motion is an illusion created by the changes in orbital speed as the Earth and other planets go around the Sun. All of the planets have retrograde cycles. Astrologically we interpret this as a time of altered perception. Traditional rules might not work. We get sidetracked. Station is the term describing the time when a planet changes back to direct or regular motion.

Retrograde Mercury
The most common and easily felt of the retrogrades, Mercury retrograde occurs about three times yearly. It is a time to learn from the past, complete old projects, reflect and reconsider. Extra rest can be needed, travel delayed, and communications diffused under this trend. There will be three retrograde Mercury cycles this year:

May 3 - May 27
in Taurus
September 4 - September 26
in Libra and Virgo
December 23 - January 12, 1997
in Capricorn

Retrograde Venus
This is the rarest of the retrogrades, but its impact is deep. Retrograde Venus is a time to be cautious and patient with decisions about love and marriage. Conservative financial moves and impeccable manners are essential. Venus will be retrograde May 20 - July 2, 1996 in Gemini.

53

ARIES

SPRING - March 21 to June 20

A reflective and secretive mood develops at the equinox. A friend or coworker shares a confidence. This draws you into a project requiring discretion. Mercury and Saturn in your 12th house are linked to this. You're kindly disposed to someone in need and will extend help and advice. Make sure your efforts are wanted and appreciated, though, before going to a great deal of extra trouble. Meditation is very helpful March 20 - 31. Listen to inner guidance to tap creativity. The Libra eclipse April 3 accents partnership and fairness. You will disrespect those who break rules and promises, but try to understand them anyway.

Saturn enters your sign April 7 to start a three-year cycle when work and responsibility are rewarding. Security needs come first. You will be deeply aware of your own strengths and weaknesses. Economize on an expenditure of time, effort, and resources. You will be energized by Mars in your own birth sign from early April through May 2. Expect to feel more enthusiastic and motivated. Outdoor exercise invigorates and revitalizes you. You assume a new aura of authority and can act in a leadership capacity. The April 17 eclipse in Aries heralds the start of a progressive time. Be alert and flexible. Success is linked to your talent for adapting to your environment. On May 4 Jupiter turns retrograde in your 10th house. Sincerity is a must at work, expand cautiously and be certain you can keep promises you make. Don't over extend. Be cautious with gambles and risks, especially if your employment is affected. June 1-14 finds Venus and the Sun nicely aspecting your 3rd house. You will communicate with charm and clarity. Write letters and make phone calls. A neighbor is kind and helpful. At the New Moon of June 15, Mars and Mercury move into a favorable sextile aspect lasting until Midsummer's Eve. Travel is uplifting and educational. Take note of new ideas which leap into your thoughts. They can be invaluable if developed in the future.

SUMMER - June 21 to Sept. 22

June 20 - July 2 old friends remember you with a quite unexpected call or visit. Your 11th house is supported with a trine between air sign planets. Become more active in clubs and organizations. An intriguing acquaintance comes from another ethnic or socioeconomic group.

July 2-15 Mercury and the Sun are in square aspect from the 4th house. It's easy to be distracted; details must be resolved before ideas will work. Home life is improved if you use humor and patience in communicating with relatives. Saturn goes retrograde in Aries the last half of July. You can relax. There is a feeling of reprieve from demanding realities and pressures. A vacation at a health spa or spiritual retreat would be worthwhile. Companions are less critical and more supportive of your ideas. They can offer hopeful inspiration. During August a T-square in the cardinal signs accents your 7th house. Follow all proprieties. Justice is important in all relationships. Connect first and foremost with people you admire and who support you. There can be differences in spiritual beliefs and values with some associates; don't try to change them. Acceptance and empathy can help you avoid confrontation. September finds Venus and Mars moving to make a soothing trine from your 5th house. Your creative talent earns admiration. A love affair is sparked, if you're receptive. A lighter work load leaves extra time to enjoy music, theater, or a movie.

AUTUMN - Sept. 23 to Dec. 20

Everything seems to be rearranging itself as the Full Moon eclipse in Aries approaches on September 26. Accept new conditions at work philosophically. Intuition can help you select the best health care. Harvest season fruits and vegetables such as apples and squash will work their magic if added to your diet. Mercury moves out of your 6th house October 9. Stress lessens and your vitality improves. Others make plans for you through October 22 while the Sun is in opposition aspect. Teamwork and compromise lead to success; it is worthwhile to examine the views voiced by others. During the week before Halloween Venus completes a quincunx. It's easier to clear away debris and get organized. Animals are supportive and sensitive companions. Set out food for stray cats or feed wild birds.

Saturn in Aries remains in a tranquil sextile aspect with Uranus throughout November. This strengthens your 1st house. You can make constructive changes. It's a good time to polish your skills. Complete work requiring analysis, precise measurements, or mathematical aptitude. New technologies and gadgets are an asset. November 15 - December 4 Mercury makes a trine from the 9th house. Make plans involving study or travel. You can acquire a deeper spiritual understanding if you look at religious practices of other lands. This is a marvelous time for writing. If you have an idea for a story or a poem put it on paper. Use new vocabulary words and add some foreign phrases if you want to be a brilliant conversationalist. Your speaking and teaching skills are in stellar form. You can change the lives of others for the better in sharing your knowledge and ideas.

From December 5 through Yule Mars moves through your 6th house and aspects Neptune. Natural healing techniques, perhaps involving herbs and music are helpful. Create a wholesome environment at work. Holiday gifts which offer comfort and healing are appreciated. If you help a coworker with a confusing situation your efforts will be remembered later.

WINTER - Dec. 21 - Mar. 20, 1997

Venus warms your 9th house with a cheerful trine for the first two weeks of winter.

Relax with a favorite book on cold evenings. Discuss travels and philosophical issues. Those you care about most will appreciate learning from and with you. Retrograde Mercury affects your job through January 12. Cope by analyzing repeated patterns and verifying instructions. It's best to postpone innovations at work. Tradition is upheld now. Older or more experienced people offer the best advice and examples. The Full Moon December 24 reveals how others love and depend upon you. You can experience heightened intuition relaxing at home.

Mid-January through February 8 planets transiting the cardinal signs create a hectic pace. Mercury is retrograde in your 10th house until January 12. Working hours may change; verify directions and schedules. Jupiter begins a sextile in your 11th house on January 22. This starts a year of really valuable friendships. You will be able to formulate goals too. At Candlemas Venus joins Jupiter in Aquarius. Ask others for help; friends appreciate your gestures of kindness and goodwill.

Mars, your ruler, goes retrograde February 6. This occurs in Libra, the zodiac sign directly opposite yours. Partners are in a turbulent phase. A mild attitude with a competitive type is best. Be aware of the past habits of others to quiet difficult issues. You can feel old associations ending and new companions becoming more important by the end of February. The eclipse in Pisces March 8 activates your 12th house. It conjoins the Sun, Mercury, and Venus. Sympathy for the needy heightens. Consider gathering warm clothes and blankets for the underprivileged and homeless or visit a friend who has been in a low cycle. Dreams are vivid during early March—the 12th house links to the subconscious mind. Try to understand your own inner psyche. Wilderness areas and outdoor beauty can enchant you March 1-15. From March 16-20 Mercury transits Aries. You will be more expressive. This quickens your wits. A problem can be solved or a new subject mastered. Be certain to follow through with travel opportunities.

TAURUS

SPRING - March 21 to June 20

The vernal equinox is welcomed by a gracious and supportive conjunction from Venus, your ruler, in your own birth sign. This benevolent pattern is in force until April 3. Your charm and agreeable manner add to the general aura of good luck just now. Invest in art, jewelry, or collectibles. Seek favors from those in authority. Romantic involvements can bring a deep happiness. The lunar eclipse April 3 affects your 6th house and will make a quincunx aspect. Adjust to conditions at work and your daily routine. Flexibility is the key to success. Your health is affected by diet, so resist tempting sweets and rich foods for the remainder of April.

During the first half of May, Jupiter and Neptune support your Sun. It's a perfect time for attending a meditation group and deepening spiritual awareness. A subject which is hard to understand suddenly is clarified if you study diligently. Mars moves through your sign during May making you energetic and competitive. Because motivation is so high, you can accomplish much. However, if anger builds, exercise restraint. Try music to restore calm.

Venus turns retrograde the 3rd week of May. This ushers in a cycle when it's easy to be sentimental and nostalgic. Enjoy memories, but remember that it's futile to live in the past. Be tolerant if someone's appearance or manners are a little rough. Humor is the best defense against vulgarity or inconsideration. May 27 - June 13 Mercury moves rapidly through your 1st house. There can be an interest in travel. It also makes you quite talkative and eloquent.

SUMMER - June 21 to Sept. 22

Your 2nd house is a focus from Midsummer's Day through Fourth of July. You will enjoy beautiful possessions and will want to hold on to all that you treasure. Shopping sprees result in important acquisitions. There is a yearning for more spending power and cash flow. Extra work which promises to compensate you well is very attractive. Your persistence and dedication are rewarded with rapid progress the last three weeks of July. The Sun makes a friendly sextile from your 3rd house July 1-22. A neighbor offers advice and suggestions. Telephone calls and letters bring insight into relationships. A short outing to a bookstore or seminar/discussion group provides provocative and inspiring ideas.

The last week of July your 4th and 10th houses are affected by Mercury, the Sun, Uranus, and a Full Moon. Family members take an interest in your professional success. Be open minded about new trends related to your work.

August opens with Mercury moving into harmony with your Sun and transit Jupiter. Your confidence and trust in others is rewarded. Companions freely share information and skills. It's a good cycle for vacation travel. Select a resort with outdoor activities or a health spa. Social events will be brightened if games of skill and strategy such as chess or even Scrabble are available.

On August 10 Pluto turns direct on your 8th house cusp. The remainder of the month is good for past life regression studies. Research goes well too. You will have new insights into the desires and motivations of others. During September Sun and Neptune aspects bring a renewed empathy with children. If you take time to teach others, your own learning deepens.

AUTUMN - Sept. 23 to Dec. 20

Mars and Venus move hand in hand through your 4th house as the harvest season begins. Take time to beautify your home and complete repair projects. The lunar eclipse in Aries September 26 activates Saturn in your 12th house. Through October 12 keep a positive mind-set as moodiness and despair threaten to complicate your life. Seek healing and inspiration from the arts or contact with nature.

October 13-29 you'll enjoy a trine from Venus. Partnerships, especially those involving business contacts, are agreeable. Your genuinely friendly and helpful concern radiates inner love. Others are responsive to you. The Full Moon in your birth sign October 26 brings new vitality into a cherished project. Extra effort on your part now leads to tangible results.

From Hallowmas through November 14 Mercury joins the Sun to create an opposition pattern. Other people have important news; you can benefit from their suggestions and experience. Be sure to compliment a friend's costume design or culinary expertise. Analyze messages coming from dreams or the spirit world. They are highly symbolic and might not be the easiest to understand.

Three planets in earth signs the last part of November favor showing your love and concern in practical ways. Prepare a nourishing dish, make a warm garment, or perform a chore for someone you care about. There is a more settled quality to closest relationships. If you have pet animals nearby, one of them bonds with you. Saturn turns direct in your 12th house as December opens. It moves into aspects with Uranus and Pluto as the days shorten into the winter's solstice. There are new alliances forming around you. Participation is healing and balancing. Teamwork now leads to recognition later.

WINTER - Dec. 21 to Mar. 20, 1997

Until January 13 retrograde Mercury in your 9th house marks a perfect time to gather photos for a keepsake album, make entries in a journal, or correspond with old friends. If you travel, return to a familiar site haunted by the happy memories of Yuletides past. This pattern peaks with the Capricorn New Moon January 8. Mars

moves into your 6th house as January begins. Neatness and organization add to contentment. You're a perfectionist just now—do all you can to relax and to release stress. Keep your workload manageable.

On January 22 Jupiter begins a long passage through your 10th house. You will become highly visible and can assume a position of leadership through the rest of the season. Contacts with foreign born and/or well-traveled and well-educated people provide a broader perspective. February finds a stellium of Aquarius placements joining the Jupiter pattern. You'll enjoy exploring ways to make a difference in your endeavors. It's a month for freshness and enthusiastic, dynamic expansion. Be daring about trying a new interest or type of work. The Aquarius New Moon February 7 can bring specifics to light.

March opens with the Sun, Mercury, and Venus in a favorable aspect from your 11th house. You will find it easier to select goals. Friends provide encouragement. You will be warmly welcomed into new circles if you seek companionship. The solar eclipse March 8 helps you to discriminate in your choice of associates. March 9-20 Mars retrogrades back into your 5th house. You will enjoy athletic and adventurous leisure time activities. An old love remembers you and could try to rekindle a flame.

GEMINI

SPRING - March 21 to June 20

An abundance of forceful energy rains on you from the ideas and choices generated by companions all year long. Pluto is in opposition to your Sun from the 7th house.

This tempts others to want to involve you in projects of great magnitude. It is a year of opportunity, but do think for yourself. Keep a balance and perspective. Work on maintaining goodwill and cooperation with others. Consider their feelings and motivations. You will discover new potentials within longtime companions. A variety of people from diverse backgrounds cross your path and add sophistication to your life.

March 20 - April 6 Saturn completes a square from your 10th house. Hard work and effort will be rewarded; put responsibility first and an important person will be impressed. Some extra sleep is the best gift you can give yourself. You've been taking on an ambitious workload and can become quite fatigued.

The first week of April Venus enters your birth sign and harmonizes with the Libra eclipse. The 1st and 5th houses are highlighted. Younger people are a delight. A hobby or creative project could lead to extra income. Mid-April is very promising for social contacts. At a party you enchant a new person with your wit and kindness. From April 17-30 the combined energies of Saturn and the eclipse path make you aware of the needs of a friend. Be helpful, yet realize you really can't take on the woes of another. Your circle of friends is beginning to shift.

May finds Mercury, your ruler, retrograde until the 27th of this month. This makes you quiet. You will prefer not to externalize your deepest thoughts and desires. Peace and privacy are cherished; quiet hours help you find your balance. Old memories and news from old contacts are in your thoughts.

In June Mars joins the Sun and Venus in your birth sign. You will enjoy physical exercise and will suddenly become more confident and assertive. This trend accelerates following the New Moon in your birth sign on June 15.

SUMMER - June 21 to Sept. 22

Midsummer's Day finds Mercurial energy flowing through your 1st house. Travel plans are finalized before July 1. You can win everyone over to your viewpoint with your exceptional persuasive skill. It's a marvelous time to make telephone calls or write. On July 2 Venus moves out of the retrograde and generates one of the best patterns for your image and appearance you've enjoyed for years. Purchase adornments and clothing; commit to a fitness routine. Music, drawing, painting, and other artistic expression can appeal to you throughout July.

August finds Pluto turning direct on the cusp of your 7th house while Mercury enters your 4th house. Your family life may be entering a new cycle. Encourage loved ones to grow. At Lammas decorate your residence with seasonal flowers and grasses. Make improvements adding to the comfort and beauty of your home. Bookshelves for your constantly expanding library would be a good place to start.

September 1-12 a Mercury-Uranus trine uplifts your 5th and 9th houses. Attend a class or lecture for valuable hints about problem solving. Television and radio programs can be unusually inspiring too. Telepathic exchanges with someone close to you demonstrate your strengthening intuition.

September 13-22 the Sun and retrograde Mercury in Virgo square you. Postpone a residential move. Investigate the terms of any new commitment before getting involved. Resist the temptation to exaggerate. A "tall tale" told now could damage your credibility. Be factual about all communication and be subtle with jokes and humor. Others may be in a serious frame of mind.

AUTUMN - Sept. 23 to Dec. 20

The lunar eclipse in Aries during the opening week of the new season aspects Saturn in your 11th house. Involvement with organizations can bring satisfaction through altruistic and humanitarian activity. You can make real progress with metaphysical and astrological studies. During the first three weeks of October the Sun makes a supportive trine which peaks with the solar eclipse in Libra on the 12th. Health improves, and your renewed vitality has a beneficial impact on creative work and social life. This is a progressive cycle. Your field of expression broadens.

The last week of October brings a Full Moon in your 12th house. Experiment with astral projection and meditation. Deeper levels of consciousness open up. You may be a bit more quiet because you are especially impressionable. You are quite psychically aware of the deepest inner feelings of others. November opens with Venus creating an upbeat aspect which is in force until the 22. Your humor and charisma win new friends. Others want to be closer. If you encourage a relationship, a commitment is offered. You can play games and win; lady luck is smiling if you want to consider a bit of adventure and speculation. The Full Moon rises in your birth sign November 24, blending nicely with Saturn, Uranus, and Pluto in early degrees of fire and air signs. Approach others with ideas the last week of the month. Be confident about taking initiative.

Mars and the Sun are both in strong, angular relationships to you from December 1 until Yule. Avoid controversy. Exercise authority in moderation. Be gentle with yourself when it comes to physical activity. Venus softens the situation from the 17th - 21st. Others show that you're loved and cherished, and you are swept into holiday forays.

WINTER - Dec. 21 to Mar. 20, 1997

The 8th house highlighted by a stellium of Capricorn planets encourages you to be discreet and private as the solstice passes. Through January 19 you will tend to investigate and analyze. There can be a new understanding of near-death experiences and your own views of the afterlife. Early January is a wonderful time to go over joint finances, also to attend to tax and insurance matters. Jupiter enters Aquarius January 22 and conjoins the transit Sun as well as Uranus. You benefit from this pattern with a friendly trine aspect in your 9th house. It's a perfect time to plan journeys for educational and spiritual purposes. Your

optimistic and expansive state of mind aids in creating marvelous opportunities through February. Teaching, public speaking, and writing can all be pursued successfully late January through February.

A volatile pattern affects your career during early March. It involves 10th house Pisces transits. The solar eclipse on March 8 makes you aware of the need for growth and adjustments. Don't attempt to hold on to the status quo. Just be conscientious about responsibilities and remain alert as well as flexible. March 9 finds retrograde Mars entering your 4th house where it will remain through March 20. Foster peace and patience at home. Ideally, you want your residence to feel safe, with the atmosphere of a peaceful sanctuary. Reconsider and postpone any major building or home improvement projects in March. March 16-20 Mercury moves into a sextile aspect. This brings you good judgment as well as valuable background information enabling you to make wise choices concerning professional or residential moves.

CANCER

SPRING - March 21 to June 20

You are touched and encouraged by the goodwill of longtime friends at the vernal equinox. The strength of your past reputation opens the path to new opportunity. This trend remains in force through April 6 with a trine from Saturn in the 9th house to your Sun. Your standard of living improves and you can acquire possessions you've yearned for. The eclipses in cardinal signs

59

during April aspect Jupiter which is in opposition to you. April 7-20 is a time to be conscientious and generous. Don't let others think for an instant you would take them for granted. When it comes to spiritual and philosophical beliefs, allow others to search for their own truth. Don't turn a conversation into a sermon.

Late April - May 1 a competitive and dynamic energy from Mars in the 10th house makes you visible at work. Use a subtle approach to those in authority. Gentle exercise is best for fitness. May 2-27 retrograde Mercury in your 11th house aspects Neptune harmoniously. Friendly calls and letters arrive from old friends. Your keen intuition assists in negotiating and sales. Those who have resisted your ideas can be won over to respond more favorably. From the end of May through June 20 retrograde Venus in your 12th house allows you to release regrets concerning a long-lost love. Kind deeds and charity are fulfilling. The gratitude expressed by those to whom you've shown kindness creates an internal euphoria. The New Moon in Gemini the week of June 15 acts as a catalyst bringing the specifics of this trend into the open.

SUMMER - June 21 to Sept. 22

Be gentle in evaluating the little shortcomings of those you admire the first week of the new season. Until June 30 the Sun is square Saturn in Aries showing tension with those in positions of authority and leadership. The first two weeks of July Mercury moves rapidly through your own birth sign making communication more pleasant. Offer suggestions, but also be a good listener. It's a perfect time for travel, especially if you can visit an island or area of historical interest.

July 16-25 a grand trine in the fire signs affects your financial indicators. You can resolve debts and find it easier to add to income. The demand for your skills intensifies, and you are aware of new options for professional growth. July 26 - Lammastide Mars moves over the Cancer cusp. You are starting a six-week cycle of tremendous energy and enthusiasm. Take some time to evaluate what you really want. It's a time to control impulses and rein in your temper. Use sunscreen and have a supply of cold drinks if you're outdoors in the summer's heat.

August 7 - September 6 Venus smiles with a conjunction to your Sun in the 1st house. Your charm and beauty are appreciated. It's a perfect time to reach out to a new love, plan a party, or express artistic inclinations. The week of August 11 Pluto turns direct exactly on your 6th house cusp, bringing empathy with animals. A pet shows love and devotion or you can interpret omens and messages from birds and other wildlife.

September 7-21 Jupiter turns direct in your 7th house. Partnerships bring growth. Those you're involved closely with open up new spheres of experience. Listen to your own inner guidance if you have the sense of being pulled into investments or other projects which seem a bit risky.

AUTUMN - Sept. 23 to Dec. 20

There is an accent on contracts, promises, and agreements the first week of the new season. Mercury turns direct with a sextile in your 3rd house. The lunar eclipse September 26 in Aries has a strong flavor of Saturn as it conjoins that planet in your 10th house. Success depends upon being realistic about what you can do. Preparation and the wise management of time are a must. Put business first and double check details to assure career stability.

October finds your 4th house accented by the Libra transits and eclipse. You can discover new facts about your family tree. Examine old diaries and photos, listen to reminiscences of old times offered by relatives. You can become more in tune with your background and all it offers you. Uranus is poised on your 8th house cusp during Halloween week. Others can ask you for financial help and advice. Old conditions and stale goals are waning. This is truly a death and rebirth trend. New realities replace old attitudes and priorities October 28 - November 2.

November 3-14 words of love are

exchanged by letter or on the phone. Mercury glides in conjunction with the Sun in your 5th house. Accept an invitation to a movie, play, or concert. Creativity accelerates if you travel or enjoy other novelty and stimulation. Study a new subject or skill if boredom threatens.

From November 15-22 Venus in aspect to Neptune can make you rather generous. Give what you can afford in terms of time and love as well as tangible support and gifts, but keep enough for yourself. Excess or misplaced generosity can be a drain.

November 22 - December 17 is an ideal time to emphasize diet and perfection. The 6th house is strong. You will find satisfaction in getting organized and developing good habits. The New Moon on December 10 crystallizes specific steps in reaching these goals. As the winter solstice approaches Mercury is close to a conjunction with Jupiter and Neptune; all three planets are in the 7th house. You'll be intensely curious about others. Psychology and social sciences captivate you. You'll meet a parade of unusual, intriguing people at holiday parties or while shopping.

WINTER - Dec. 21 to Mar. 20, 1997

You're noticed and appreciated the first week of winter. The Full Moon December 24 is in Cancer. This makes it easier for you to enlist help and elicit responses. The last week of December brings spiritual awakening through dreams and meditation. Seeking the perfect home and family life will be a focus in January. Mars begins a passage through your 4th house. You could redecorate, remodel, or even sell a home. Relatives can be restless; allow loved ones plenty of freedom.

Positive financial twists are promised January 22 - February 15. Jupiter, entering Aquarius and your 8th house, conjoins the transit Sun and Uranus. An investment or legacy adds to your earnings. You have an awareness of what true wealth really is. Material values are balanced with a respect for the intangible riches such as love and a healthy life. Until February 26 the influ-

ence of Venus can add a possessive, intense note to love. Share a bit of humor and be understanding with your nearest and dearest.

March 1-9 you will have a zest for adventure and travel. There are Pisces planets in your 9th house elevating your thoughts. The Pisces solar eclipse March 8 brings in opportunity for you to be on the go. A visit to a school, library, or spiritual center can illuminate and uplift you. March 10-20 imported foods or ethnic clothing are enjoyable. Love assumes an abstract quality. You would appreciate an exciting and imaginative companion with whom to share adventures.

LEO

SPRING - March 21 to June 20

Personal involvements will be electric, exciting, and unpredictable all year long. Uranus in opposition aspect to your Sun from the 7th house generates this trend, and it is a powerful one. You can meet people who revolutionize your whole life. Allow others freedom and recognize when a relationship must move and grow. The April 3 eclipse in your 3rd house smooths communications with a pleasant sextile aspect; gather information and be a good listener.

Saturn crosses into your 9th house April 7 where it will trine you through the rest of the year. It's a marvelous time to look at educational travel, perhaps to a site of spiritual significance. Progress is made with studies. You can master an important subject or complete a degree program. The solar eclipse in Aries April 17 brings the specifics into focus.

You will be ambitious and competitive as May Eve passes. Mars and Mercury energize your 10th house throughout May. You are motivated and enthused at work, but diplomacy and patience are a must to assure success. Near the Full Moon on May 3 separate family and personal issues from professional responsibilities.

June is a time to develop nurturing friendships. Venus and the Sun are sextile from the 11th house, adding to your charm and popularity. However, Venus' retrograde motion makes you responsive to peer pressure, especially from those who are in pursuit of all kinds of pleasure. Enjoy yourself as the solstice approaches, but do keep your goals and priorities in sight. The New Moon June 15 is supportive of positive resolutions.

SUMMER - June 21 to Sept. 22

June 20 - July 1 brings a rare opportunity to adjust the decisions and actions linked to the past. Five planets are retrograde in areas of the chart which tie to the closure of old relationships. July 2-15 the Sun and Mercury polarize Jupiter and Neptune in the 12th and 6th houses. You have an intuitive understanding of animals and nature. Spend some time in meditation while sitting on the ground or standing braced against a tree. Inner healing and a sense of peace will be generated. Service to others and to the planet brings you a profound happiness. Visit an ill or elderly person or clear away debris from a park or seaside.

From July 16-31 your confident and dramatic way of expressing ideas wins supporters. Mercury moves rapidly through your birth sign. It's a marvelous time to write letters, make calls. Your efforts at sales, public speaking, or acting succeed far beyond all expectations. During August your 12th house is highlighted by Venus and Mars in Cancer. This gives a flair for strategy and subtle action. Your birthday finds you introspective. You are able to cherish your secrets and privacy, even those closest to you know only what you want to reveal. August is a favorable time to work with affirmations and visualization.

September begins with Jupiter turning direct in your 6th house. Health is improving, and you can discover herbal or other natural remedies to enhance well-being on the 1-6. On September 7 Venus enters Leo. Summer's end is one of the happiest times all year. September 7-22 you can arrange a party to celebrate the season with your nearest and dearest friends and family. There is opportunity to pursue cultural, social, and artistic interests. A romance becomes more stable. There is a deeper sense of intimacy with those you truly love.

AUTUMN - Sept. 23 to Dec. 20

You will extend initiative and assume authority. Mars is in your sign until October 29. This is a time of powerful accomplishment, but you must focus on the highest values and goals. Mars is like fire, capable of great destruction if mishandled, but warming and uplifting if used positively. If you sense you're overbearing or expecting too much, pull back. Exercise adds to your overall well-being. The eclipse September 26 awakens you to new values and philosophies. Travel may be complicated near that date though. If possible, stay in familiar territory September 26-30. October 12-21 the eclipse in Libra combined with the Sun and Mercury in the 3rd house makes you restless. New places and new ideas would refresh you. Purchase a couple of newly published books or vary the routes you travel and see the neighborhood from a different perspective. Variety is a must.

Halloween finds your 4th house highlighted. Decorate your home with seasonal motifs. Make repairs and organize the household to generate domestic harmony. Acquiring security and generating more income will be in your thoughts November 1-14. You will be protective of people as well as possessions you're attached to because Mars crosses into your 2nd house while aspecting Pluto.

November 15-30 is a cycle of clarity in understanding your deepest loves and attachments. Mercury and Pluto trine your

Sun from the 5th house bring a transcendent quality to affections. You can make a difference for the better in the lives of those you care for, especially in the case of younger people.

December finds you applying spiritual teachings to daily life situations. Saturn turns direct in your 9th house; it forms trines with your Sun and the Sagittarius planets. The result is a fortunate grand trine pattern in force until Yule. You'll be vital and creative. Your appearance improves, lending strength to your self-esteem. This results in good fortune affecting personal life as well as professional status. The New Moon December 10 marks a week of good social opportunities and cheer. December 15-20 Venus moves into harmony with the whole pattern. Ask others for help and express your love openly. You will meet with deep and loving acceptance.

WINTER - Dec. 21 to Mar. 20, 1997

Keep your schedule and environment wholesome as the solstice passes. Mercury turns retrograde in your 6th house and health could need a bit of attention. Use a fireplace, bright lights, and hot drinks to chase away gloom and chills. A few extra hours of sleep is the best holiday gift to give yourself December 22-31.

January is a time to be subtle and appreciate being in the background. Recognize that there is a power in discretion and silence. Cardinal sign planets create an aspect pattern which vents into your 12th house. Patience helps with any difficult people. The Full Moon in Leo January 23 alters the mood of the New Year. Vitality is renewed, and you're more positive. Support and recognition come as January ends. As February opens you start to feel the impact of Jupiter starting a year-long cycle in your 7th house. Partnerships are growing. Others want commitment from you. Mercury joins Jupiter from February 9-27. Encourage others to communicate; conversations and letters help you explore the parameters of important relationships.

March 1-20 is an ideal time to examine financial documents and decisions. Investments, insurance coverage, and taxes can be dealt with efficiently. The eclipse pattern in your 8th house, coupled with Mars retrograde in the 2nd, allows you to purge any old financial debts or dilemmas. A sense of dèjá vu surrounds you in March. You're deeply aware of interconnections between the present and other lives at other times.

VIRGO

SPRING - March 21 to June 20

Communication is a delicate matter as the new season starts. Make every effort to understand and respect the views of others. Pisces planets oppose your Sun from the 7th house at the vernal equinox. Moderation is the best policy to adopt in your expectations of others. On April 7 this pattern passes. Mercury and Jupiter in your sister earth signs of Taurus and Capricorn are favorable April 8-18. They support your 5th and 9th houses. Travel and educational activities are captivating. You can learn from leisure time pursuits. A romantic tryst with a very sophisticated and talented individual is likely.

On April 17 the eclipse makes you aware of your own deepest needs and desires. You can sense a past life link to the current range of experiences. April concludes with aspects from Mars and Neptune in force. Dreams are a key to messages from your higher mind. If food or medicine is a theme in those dreams, check the environment for chemicals and pollutants. They can affect you.

May is a wonderful month for making

adjustments and suggestions at work. A mutual reception between Venus and Mercury is nicely supported by the Sun in Taurus the 1-20. You'll enjoy a new perspective on old puzzles and problems. It is easier to view bittersweet memories with appreciation and understand why certain situations occured. The Full Moon on May 3 promises a week of abundant calls and letters; it affects your 3rd house just as Mercury turns retrograde. Timely responses are appreciated by others. Reassuring words from you assure security and goodwill. May 21-31 Venus retrograde interacts with four outer planet retrogrades. Keep up with prior commitments at work to protect your credibility. Complete projects in progress before considering new directions.

June 1-12 music heals and energizes you. A Mercury-Neptune pattern shows exceptional sensitivity to sound. Play an ocharina or drum or dance spontaneously to a favorite recording. Bird songs and the voices of the wind and sea speak volumes to you. June 13-20 four Gemini planets including Mars in the 10th house awaken ambitions. You are competitive and can accomplish much related to career.

SUMMER - June 21 to Sept. 22

Keep the overall goals and perspective in mind regarding work June 20-30. You're feeling a double quincunx pattern with Saturn and Uranus. Your own mind-set creates much of what is happening. Notes of humor and lightness are more effective with associates than an overbearing or severe manner.

July begins with a cheerful sextile from Mercury and the Sun in your 11th house. You'll enjoy witty, talkative friends. Accept an opportunity to do public speaking or teaching. You'll enjoy involvement with book clubs or other organizations that help you to learn July 1-15. Saturn begins a retrograde pattern in your 8th house the last half of the month. It's a perfect time for serious pursuit of metaphysical studies linked to the afterlife and reincarnation. Questions about expense accounts and investments can come up; keep all receipts and financial records in order.

August brings a fascination with spiritual healing or the latest vitamin and nutrition theories. From August 1-25 Mercury moves through your birth sign making a trine to Jupiter and Neptune. Travels lead to improvement in your quality of life, especially if the destination is over or near water. The last week of August the Full Pisces Moon in your 7th house lets others express feelings about you. Partnerships reach a turning point.

Financial decisions and choices need attention September 1-12. Mercury in your 2nd house turns retrograde oppose Saturn. Don't try to force your values on those who aren't receptive. Associates are rather conservative. Clip coupons and comparison shop for the best prices when making purchases. September 13 through the eve of the equinox Venus and Mars are gliding together in your 12th house. Your sincere compassion for another wins you a new friend. You will make kind, generous gestures toward those less fortunate. Favors you perform now will be returned later.

AUTUMN - Sept. 23 to Dec. 20

You will display a flair for research and detective work September 22-30. The lunar eclipse path lights your 8th house near September 26. It draws a mystery into the open. Your desires can be directed toward making a special acquisition or into establishing a personal relationship.

Venus moves into your own birth sign as October opens. This is the time to reach out to those you love and admire. Purchase finery in preparation for Hallowmas celebrations and experiment with artistic expression October 1-29. The solar eclipse on October 12 affects your 2nd house. Your overall attitude toward money and material values is shifting. There can be a new demand for your job skills; explore employment possibilities during the week following the eclipse. October ends with Mars entering Virgo. You'll enjoy outdoor exercise and will feel quite competitive from October 30 on. Your enthusiasm and added energy makes others turn to you for inspiration and leadership as the season progresses.

November sees you looking for ways to improve and protect your home. Pluto in the 4th house is activated by mutable sign transits. You can add new members to your extended family and have a deepening of insight into your childhood. November 24 - December 4 you will look critically at your residence. A move or a remodeling and redecorating plan is almost irresistible. On December 5 Mercury approaches a friendly conjunction with Neptune and Jupiter in your 5th house. Until Yule your social life is enlivened by invitations and visits. You can impress an admirer with a kind word or note. If you want to make holiday gifts, try penning an original story or poem. Vacation travel is relaxing and delightful through December 21.

WINTER - Dec. 21 to Mar. 20, 1997

Protect yourself from chills and confusion by planning a simple schedule until January 13. Your ruling planet Mercury is retrograde until then. Extra rest is a must. Venus joins Mercury in the 5th house on January 10. An old love can be fondly remembered or even rejuvenated.

During January children surprise you with a display of kindness or creativity. Jupiter begins a year-long transit through Aquarius January 22. This benefits your health as it draws benevolent forces into your 6th house. You can treat an old illness or establish a more wholesome daily routine. Late January until February 18 pets are especially important; they provide a new level of comfort and companionship.

The February 22 Full Moon is in Virgo. The 22-28 is an emotion-charged week. You're expressive and especially sensitive. Promising contacts can be made as people notice and respond to you.

March 1-15 others are preoccupied and distracted. Be patient if you have to repeat questions or wait for phone calls to be returned. Mercury is in opposition from your 7th house, showing associates have different thoughts and conflicting information. Observe facial expressions and body

language to aid in communication. The season finishes with a Mars retrograde in your own birth sign March 9-20, it trines Neptune. Strategy and the use of intuition help you to win others to your viewpoint. Your beloved is easier to understand. You can guide the course of a close relationship.

LIBRA

SPRING - March 21 to June 20

Invest in purchases which bring you joy and beauty while they appreciate in value. Jewels or art are some good examples. Spring begins with Venus well-aspected in Taurus in your 8th house. Profits as well as pleasures come through the purchases of antiques or luxuries. The April 3 eclipse at the Full Moon in your own birth sign ushers in a time of endings and new cycles. The eclipse is conjunct the Moon's North Node so it will, according to ancient astrology traditions, leave you in better condition in the end. Keep in mind that change is growth. Be receptive to the idea of a new job or residence this year.

The Sun, Mars, and Saturn are all in your 7th house April 7-19. Be alert to the needs and expectations of others. Adapt to the trends partners set to avoid friction. Social sciences such as psychology fascinate you. As May Eve approaches you will feel the support of a trine from Venus in your 9th house. Art and music from other lands can create a spiritual climate. Travel to places of cultural diversity would be wonderful April 18 - May 2. If that is impractical, try reading literature or watching educational films accenting other customs and countries.

After May 3 you may be a little perplexed about the financial decisions and attitudes of others. If you feel unsettled or disappointed about this, investigate a bit. Understanding can help. Mars and retrograde Mercury quincunx you from the 8th house. Expressing deepest desires and passions can alter your life now. Think of long-range consequences if you feel swept along by feelings or compulsions. The New Moon in Taurus May 17 brings a peak to the pattern.

June finds Venus, your ruler, retrograde. A deeper understanding of your background and past decisions develops. Brush up on etiquette and social niceties June 1-13. From June 14-20 a stellium of the Sun and three planets in your 9th house elevates your consciousness. You will be receptive to learning and new ideas.

SUMMER - June 21 to Sept. 22

At Midsummer a trend begins at work which encourages you to use more authority and become more visible. Until July 1 the Sun and Saturn are in square aspect affecting you in a dynamic way. Venus moves out of retrograde motion just after the Full Moon the first week of July. Your vitality improves and the environment is more nurturing. A loved one helps you reach a cherished goal. A memorable gathering with family and friends highlights July 1-15 happily.

July 16-31 Mercury in your 11th house forms trines with retrograde Saturn and Pluto. It's easy to forgive and forget old hurts. This is a time to build healthy relationships. Call a friend you'd like to get to know better or become more active in clubs and groups. August opens with Mars, Jupiter, and Saturn forming a dramatic pattern in cardinal signs. Your life is very exciting. Get organized and pour effort into the most important priorities. You can discover a new talent or aptitude and surprise yourself as well as others. Venus changes signs August 7 and intermingles with the other transits through the end of the month. This makes you glamorous and charismatic as you express new abilities. There is friendship at work which could transform into a romantic liaison by September 5.

September opens with Mercury in Libra turning retrograde and moving back into Virgo. From September 1-11 listen carefully in conversation, reread directions. Clarity of understanding is a must. September 12-22 Mars and Venus in Leo form a gentle 11th house sextile. Relationships are smoothed; it is easier to define your goals. Politics and community activities can captivate you. A progressive and helpful mood develops.

AUTUMN - Sept. 23 to Dec. 20

September 22-26 analyze what is holding you back from making your daily life exactly as you want. Pluto makes an exact sextile to Uranus affecting your 3rd house. You discover the solution to a long-standing blockage or problem. The lunar eclipse September 26 starts a two-week pattern when people around you are in transit. Openings at work and changes in status open you to new options. Follow laws and rules conscientiously.

October 9-26 Mercury moves rapidly through your own sign of Libra. Your mental attitude is more positive. Your confidence and concern inspire others to seek your advice. A group discussion can be especially fruitful in providing information and ideas. The eclipse in your birth sign October 12 outlines your options and illustrates what is most important. Health and fitness programs are worth exploring. Add fresh fruits, herbal teas, and stretching exercises to your day to assure the best quality of life.

From October 13-29 you cherish time alone. Seclusion brings peace. Venus in your 12th house aspects Neptune. Subtle mystical energies are coming into play. As Halloween approaches you can plan a pilgrimage to a place of spiritual significance or use color and music to add loveliness to the environment.

October 30 - November 22 Venus moves through your own sign. It's the perfect time to purchase clothes and take care of your appearance. You are radiant and vibrant. Ask others for favors and develop new contacts. Love and admiration are on the upswing. November ends with three planets in your 3rd house, including Mercury. A neighbor or sibling is expressive and would relish a conversation with you. You can find newspapers, radio, and television especially stimulating; there is a desire to keep up with current events.

December is a time to be realistic about relationships and commitments. Saturn turns direct in your 7th house the first week of the month. Pull away from links that inhibit or discourage you. Strengthen those which you know have potential for the future. December 8-21 Mercury joins Neptune and Jupiter in your 4th house. New insights about your heritage surface. Early photos or old diaries can be revealing. Seasonal candles and other decorations create an especially powerful atmosphere at home. Fragrance is healing and enriching. Try aromatherapy with incense or potpourri. Myrrh, bayberry, pine, or cedar are ideal choices.

WINTER - Dec. 21 to Mar. 20, 1997

Patience is a must December 21 - January 2. The solar transit activates cardinal sign planets in opposition and square to you. This sparks a competitive mood. If you sense some jealousy or anger coming from a coworker or relative, rise above it. Mars enters your birth sign January 3 where it will remain through the first week of March. This brings you the gifts of enthusiasm, energy, and motivation. Accomplishment accelerates early in the New Year. Winter sports and games are a source of delight and healthful exercise.

You will make leisure hours productive from January 22 - February 19. First Jupiter and the Sun, then Mercury and Venus join Uranus in Aquarius. This is very beneficial for creative and cultural pursuits. News of a friend's nuptials can bring joy. Between Candlemas and Valentine's Day your own social calendar is alive with attractive invitations. A court-

ship may ensue. February culminates with others depending upon you to make daily routine more agreeable. The application of your natural genius for diplomacy helps.

March 1-15 three planets in your 6th house are energized by the eclipse in Pisces. Health care options fascinate you. News about spiritual healing, miracle vitamins, and alternative therapies is a focus. Stress levels can build now, so laugh at little problems and take time to relax.

March 16-20 you are newly aware of how important you are to others. Mercury moves to oppose you generating a series of calls, letters, and suggestions.

SCORPIO

SPRING - March 21 to June 20

There is a steady, secure quality about love as springtime begins. Venus smiles on your 7th house of marriage and partnerships through April 2. The April 3 eclipse in your 12th house tends to bring secrets out. You will have to cope with an exposed, vulnerable feeling early in the month. As April progresses you'll be absorbed in routine work and performing helpful services. A meticulous approach to details wins you admiration April 7-20. Saturn, Mars, and the Sun all form a quincunx from Aries and the 6th house.

April 21-30 is a perfect time for promotional and public relations work. You catch the attention of others with the feelings you infuse into conversations and letters. The exceptional communication talent is generated by Mercury and the Sun in

Taurus in opposition aspect. That combination allows you to affect the hearts and minds of others.

On May 3 the Full Moon is in Scorpio. Throughout the first week of May expect some vivid and symbolic dreams. Beltane rites help you to recognize which people and circumstances are positive. Draw closer to them. Emotional energy provides stamina. May 8-28 retrograde Mercury and Mars aspect you by opposition. Other people are dynamic. They have numerous plans and ideas. Sift through these with care as all of them might not be workable. It is a good idea to verify appointments. Forget adversaries from the past. Refuse to give them any more attention.

May 29 - June 14 there is a universal desire for peace and goodwill. Conflicts are overcome through compromise as you enjoy beneficial energy from Neptune and the Taurus transits. June 15-20 investigations give you a new perspective on associates and family members. A quincunx pattern involving the Sun and three Gemini planets could provide more information about others than you want. Karmic issues are clearly defined and you can resolve old patterns.

SUMMER - June 21 to Sept. 22

Love attachments undergo a catharsis from Midsummer's Eve through July 2 when Venus completes a retrograde in your 8th house. You discover how to rise above jealousy or insecurity to bring a more transcendent and supportive quality to love. The Blue Moon June 30 helps you to express your feelings with special eloquence. It conjoins Jupiter in your 3rd house.

July 3-15 Mercury dashes quickly through your 9th house. It's an ideal time for travel. If unable to vacation now, make plans for a future journey. You'll be drawn to reading too and can find pleasure frequenting your favorite bookstore or library. July 16-31 be sensitive to messages from your body. Saturn goes retrograde in your health sector. This promises an opportunity to correct any physical weaknesses and resolve health issues.

August is a month of accomplishment. Mars supports your Sun with a trine giving strength and a sense of purpose. On the 7th Venus joins Mars in Cancer and underscores the favorable pattern. You can make friends with foreign-born people. Instinctively you will know what to say and do to win support for your views and projects. Pluto, ruler of Scorpio, leaves a long retrograde on August 10. Past obligations melt away. It is easier to enjoy the present and plan for the future. The August 28 Full Moon brings delight in the company of younger people. A child you're close to seems very grown up.

September 1-11 there can be schemes and subtleties involved in communication passed your way. Get both sides of all stories before making decisions involving others. From deep inside your subconscious comes an array of visions and daydreams. These can be inspiration for creative work. Mercury turns retrograde in your 12th house.

September 12-22 you will attract attention from successful individuals whom you admire. These connections are helpful in seeking career guidance. Venus and Mars link in the 10th house bringing enthusiasm as well as pleasure to the pursuit of professsional aspirations.

AUTUMN - Sept. 23 to Dec. 20

Closer friendships develop with people you meet through vocations or avocations. Plans are discussed for the future with a focus on humanitarian, scientific, or metaphysical goals. This continues through October 8 with Mercury completing a sextile aspect in your 11th house. October 9-25 the eclipse along with Sun and Mercury transits highlight your 12th house. Prepare for the new season carefully. It is better to say too little than too much about sensitive topics. Your inner spiritual quest is strong— you're introspective and reflective. The Full Moon in Taurus October 26 brings a shift and you will be more inclined to share and express ideas through Halloween.

November 1-14 the Sun and Mercury in your own birth sign sextile Jupiter in the

3rd house. You have self-confidence and marvelous persuasive talent. Enlist support and seek information. Word skills are in top form. You can produce impressive writing and speak eloquently. Follow through with travel opportunities. It's one of the best cycles all year for vacation or business trips. The Scorpio New Moon November 10 brings clarity and focus.

November concludes with an awareness of how the meaning of money and security is shifting. Mercury joins your ruling planet Pluto in the 2nd house. You're aware of what money can and can't do and of what you value most. November 23 - December 16 Venus is in your sign of Scorpio. This promises improvement in your quality of life. It's the best time to make holiday season purchases and schedule parties. You enjoy love and admiration.

December 17-21 appeals and requests from others affect you. The Sun is square Mars touching your 2nd and 11th houses. Offer practical assistance to others, but try to help them help themselves. Include crystals or favorite stones on your Yule altar to make the most of this fiery, yet earthy pattern.

WINTER - Dec. 21 to Mar. 20, 1997

Making a game out of chores or adding humor to lighten a conversation which is becoming intense will be natural as the new season begins. The Sun and three planets make a bright sextile in your 3rd house. There is a new alertness and cleverness to your perceptions. Review language skills and other studies. Something which seemed hard to grasp before is now less elusive. This trend continues through January 19. The Full Moon December 24 is very favorably placed at a trine to your Sun. 1996 ends with warmth and harmony on the increase. Add an evening of art, theater, or music to end-of-the-year celebrations.

Comfort factors at home are in your thoughts the last ten days of January. Aquarius planets are in your 4th house. You will relish a roomier, improved residence. You could seek a new apartment or schedule home improvements before the

end of February. Venus joins the Sun and Jupiter on February 3 to remain in your 4th house through February 26. Plan a gathering with relatives or purchase art and furniture for your home. There is a new aura of love and contentment coming into your residence and family life. Near Valentine's Day you will feel a square from Mercury. Be kind and tactful when conversing with loved ones. It's better to speak less and listen more.

March begins happily with trine aspects in your 5th house from the Sun, Mercury, and Venus in Pisces. March 1-7 there is rapport with those you care for most. Communicate your deepest desires and concerns; you will be understood. March 8-19 Mars retrogrades over the Libra cusp back to Virgo where it will oppose the Pisces transits. You will feel this with some diided loyalties among friends. Remain impartial if there are conflicts and competitive feelings brewing. A liberal and tolerant attitude carries you a long way as the winter wanes.

SAGITTARIUS

SPRING - March 21 to June 20

The entire year finds you in the midst of major changes in self-awareness. Your will power is increasing, you are more daring and purposeful than ever before. In many ways you're going through a renaissance. All of this is promised by Pluto as it moves through your birth sign toward a conjunction with your Sun. March 20-24 Mars squares the Sun. Get into shape slowly for outdoor exercise or yardwork—don't overdo. March 25 - April 6 Saturn completes a square with your Sun. Established patterns change slowly; old memories can be haunting. Let time be a healer. Patience with elderly people and authority figures is essential.

April's eclipses fall in the houses of love and friendship. You will experience sudden meetings and partings. The roles others play in your life are chameleon-like. Creative gifts are evident April 7-18. April 19 - May 1 you will enjoy an energizing Mars trine. Follow fresh ideas and take the initiative. Games and contests captivate you; you can compete to win now. Beltane through May 19 your 6th house is a focus. Select a healthy menu and create a wholesome atmosphere. Be sensitive to factors that contribute to your wellness and incorporate them into your daily schedule. June 1 brings a Full Moon in your own sign of Sagittarius. This draws vivid dreams and insights. Your emotions and desires are strong. Maintain balance. You attract attention and can win support for a favorite project if you reach out to others during the first half of June.

On June 13 Mars begins an opposition aspect. The Sun combines forces with this through June 20. Other people are dynamic and forceful. Some associates will carry you forward with their warmth and enthusiasm. If you sense aggression, though, back away.

SUMMER - June 21 to Sept. 22

Midsummer's Day through July 1 be tolerant if others are inattentive. There is a general air of being preoccupied which interferes with deep concentration. Divide work hours into small segments to make the best of this trend. July 2-22 detective and occult or thriller themes in movies and books are engrossing. An 8th house quincunx from the Sun attracts you to subcultures and mysteries. Accept your financial situation philosophically. It is essential that you enjoy what you have and not live beyond your means. Use caution with charge cards and avoid borrowing.

July 23-31 a grand trine in your element, fire, comes into play. It's a perfect time for vacation travel or to consider study

programs. Your workload is lighter and you resolve problems with grace and ease.

With Lammastide Mercury crosses into your 10th house. Much is expected of you. Others rely on your skills. The role of guide and teacher is yours throughout August. Pluto completes its retrograde August 10. You realize that week that a part of the past must end. You will want to be unencumbered. The August 28 Full Moon in your 4th house makes you appreciate your family and home. Relatives respond if you express your love.

The first week of September Jupiter, your ruler, finishes a retrograde in your money house. The financial situation is about to brighten considerably. Debts or other drains on your resources diminish. You would be well paid if you seek extra work. September 8-22 there can be marvelous social prospects with foreign-born or well-traveled friends. Be friendly if on a journey now. There can be meetings with kindly and valuable people. Studies progress well. Enroll in seminars and classes. Venus and Mars in Leo shine in your 9th house. Writing and publishing would be favored too.

AUTUMN - Sept. 23 to Dec. 20

People offer advice and assistance. Human interest values such as friendship are worth more than business acumen. A sextile from the Sun in your 11th house starts at the equinox. On September 26 the eclipse in your 5th house promises a week of surprises revolving around love. Use care in establishing a new relationship.

October 4-27 Venus in Virgo makes a square to your Sun. Resist the temptation to socialize, play jokes or games at work. Put business first. It's not the time to procrastinate; protect the reputation you've worked to establish. The eclipse on October 12 finds peer pressure strong. Avoid danger. Keep good company.

October 28-31 create a personal and natural Halloween altar with gourds and seasonal grasses. Add candles for inspiration in meditation. Mercury crosses into your 12th house, showing your state of mind benefits from peace and quiet and simplicity.

November 1-14 a charitable gesture or two makes you more happy within. Be a true friend; put the welfare of others first. You will be rewarded. Venus in your 11th house indicates this. November 15 - December 4 Mercury moves through your sign. You will examine and discuss new ideas. Useful information comes your way. This can tie directly to employment or an avocation. An impromptu journey provides a welcome break. December 5-21 earthy values come into play with Capricorn and Virgo planets in your 2nd and 10th houses. You will want to acquire and protect possessions. Goals selected on the New Moon in your sign December 10 link to security. On the 17th Venus enters your own sign of Sagittarius. Saturnalia through Yule holiday celebrations abound. You are a sought-after guest. Take special care with your appearance. Seasonal dances and music can be especially enjoyable.

WINTER - Dec. 21 to Mar. 20, 1997

Pleasures and delights brighten the dark, cold days now. December 21 - January 9 Venus is still in your sign. You can revel in holiday greetings and gifts. A new admirer you met near your birthday becomes a closer pal. On January 10 the mood shifts. A stellium of planets in your 2nd house sets the pace. Thoughts and conversations revolve around practical considerations and contributions you can make. During the last ten days of January, three Aquarius placements including Jupiter create a smooth sextile in your 3rd house. It's a good time for letters, calls, and dealings with the media. Your skills in negotiation can win needed support. A neighbor may involve you in a community program.

February finds Venus and Mercury moving to conjunct your ruling planet, Jupiter. Through the 12th meditation and spiritual circles offer you new philosophies and insights. You are sensitive to sound and color and can excel at artistic expression or musical performance. February 13-28 retrograde Mars aspects Pluto

in Sagittarius. This can make you aware of how you have used time and resources. Thoughts center on future wishes and goals. Pull away from associates who have complicated your life in the past.

The first two weeks of March the sector of home and family life is strenghtened by the Sun, Mercury, and Venus. You might initiate a family gathering or redecorate and improve the house. The New Moon March 8 brings appreciation for your family background. Pluto turns retrograde in your sign that week also. You will be able to draw on hidden reserves of strength and memories to acquire independence.

Winter ends with Mercury joining Saturn in your 5th house March 16-20. Practical, constructive use of leisure time will add to your happiness. Working or studying can be satisfying. You're not in a frivolous frame of mind.

CAPRICORN

SPRING - March 21 to June 20

Your charisma and charm are blossoming with the coming of spring. Through April 2 Venus blesses you with a trine from your 5th house. This brings invitations and makes you the recipient of many unexpected kindnesses.

On April 3 the lunar eclipse generates surprises in your 10th house of career. Be flexible at work and look upon new conditions with a positive attitude. By April 17 there is a great deal of activity in your 4th house of home and family. Mars and Saturn combine with an eclipse in that sector. A new residence can look very attractive.

Family members are moving forward in their lives. Give them support and good wishes as May Eve approaches.

May opens with Jupiter, the largest, luckiest planet of all, in the middle of your own sign of Capricorn. The Sun and Mercury and, after May 3, Mars trine you. Take a risk or play some games of chance. Your horizons are widening. Jupiter turns retrograde May 4. This begins a four-month healing trend. You can right old wrongs and recover from regrets. Wisdom and benefits gleaned from past experiences help with present decisions. On May 20 the Sun joins Venus in your 6th house. Pets provide healing and companionship. May 20 - June 12 is a perfect time to adopt a new animal friend. Get organized—an orderly schedule and neatness enhance your well-being and productivity. June 12-20 Mercury and Mars also enter your 6th house as they cross into Gemini. Look at your diet and exercise programs. It is an ideal time to implement new health habits. You will feel an urge to be productive. Your job and projects bring deep satisfaction.

SUMMER- June 21 to Sept. 22

Cooperation and consideration are a must June 21-30. The Sun and Saturn are in square aspect affecting your 4th and 7th houses. This makes you aware of how important relationships are. Take time to reinforce and maintain them. The Blue Moon falls late on June 30 in your own birth sign. Spend that evening with meditations and affirmations. Magical workings can take effect in delightful and unexpected ways during the two weeks following the lunation. Record and interpret dreams with care during this time as well. Venus turns direct in your 6th house on July 2. You will find coworkers more mannerly after that. Personal situations at work are resolved amicably. July 3-18 the Sun aspects Neptune in Capricorn by opposition. This brings a series of charming but eccentric people your way. Verify information you're given. There is an illusional quality to your perceptions of others. Good or bad, they might not be accurate. The

New Moon July 15 in your opposing sign of Cancer highlights specifics.

July 16-31 Mercury moves rapidly through Leo affecting your 8th house by quincunx. You can enjoy a bit of escapism. Metaphysical literature and spiritual studies, especially those with a focus on the afterlife, can intrigue you. You could also be drawn to romantic adventure or espionage thrillers. You will feel power and strength through being a bit discreet, just smile if others accuse you of being secretive. Keep your mystery.

August promises to be competitive. Mars is in opposition to your Sun all month. Cooperate with others but back away from those who are too aggressive. It's best not to make too many demands. September 3 Jupiter turns direct in Capricorn. A time of great progress and growth begins with the harvest season. As September begins, the Sun affects your 9th house. Well-educated people and travel opportunities are positive elements in your life. It's a marvelous time for writing, public speaking, reading, or enrollment in classes.

AUTUMN - Sept. 23 to Dec. 20

Late September encourages you to be realistic about family dynamics. Saturn is in your 4th house, the September 26 eclipse in Aries is conjunct. New trends and the status quo can be out of balance. Use existing supplies and recycle old items to conserve on expenses. Elderly and very young relatives have new thoughts and needs. Communicate with them.

October brings several transits to the top of your birth chart spanning the 9th, 10th, and 11th houses. You will be more visible at work and within organizations and groups. Present programs at gatherings, be a leader. New events around you make an opening for your progress near the eclipse in Libra October 12. October 13-25 Venus and Neptune are in a trine in earth signs. You can express beauty and love through music, color, and poetry. Art appreciation is favored too. Nature's beauty heals and uplifts you. Take time to focus on animals and the outdoors as Hallowmass approaches. October 26 - November 13 a sextile from Mercury favors sales and negotiations. Agreements reached are mutually acceptable. The last half of November a strong accent on the three fire signs emphasizes inner growth. Be introspective about your own motivations; act on what feels comfortable and is supported by your inner guidance.

The first week of December Saturn, your ruler, completes a retrograde pattern. You will feel more settled with home and family issues. You will realize what your heritage and family background means. Make the most of your inherited traits and early teachings. December 5-20 Mercury joins Neptune and Jupiter in your birth sign. You will feel a sense of hope and encouragement. Prophetic insights are revealing; your optimistic, confident use of words will draw others to you. This is a favorable time for either holiday or business travel.

WINTER - Dec. 21 to Mar. 20, 1997

This Yuletide favors following traditional celebrations. Mercury is retrograde in your sign until January 12. Expect calls and visits from beloved friends. The Full Moon in Cancer December 24 brings renewal of old involvements. Those closest to you reveal innermost desires. Be receptive to holiday plans a loved one suggests. There could be a birthday celebration or other serendipitous pleasures in store for you. The Capricorn New Moon January 8 marks a week when you can make resolutions and start new projects to unfold during the year ahead. Venus sweeps through your own birth sign January 10 - February 2. Make wardrobe choices; new finery will be especially flattering if selected now. You have friends and admiration. Put effort into new relationships.

February brings a group of planets in your 2nd house, including a Jupiter-Uranus conjunction in Aquarius. You may have a changing attitude about income and security. There is a new awareness about what money really does and doesn't mean. New technologies and skills can link to

your employment. Be ready to grow, expand, and experiment to assure success. On February 9 Mercury joins the other planets in Aquarius. This promises you information about and an understanding of financial matters. Conversations revolve around business until the end of the month.

From March 1-8 you can do a great deal of writing. Cards and letters as well as stories and poems flow freely. Neighbors are more friendly; accept invitations they extend. Return telephone calls promptly. They can be very important near the time of the eclipse March 8. Your 3rd house is energized by Pisces planets in a sextile aspect.

March 9-20 time alone in meditation and reflection is precious. Pluto turns retrograde in your 12th house, pulling you away from groups and crowds. Mars in your 9th house brings you in touch with those who have different values. Acceptance of those who have conflicting attitudes and priorities is a must. From March 16-20 listen to others, but don't waste precious time and energy on argument.

AQUARIUS

SPRING - March 21 to June 20

You are in a time of expanding consciousness, greater self-expression, and heightened awareness. All year long Uranus, your ruling planet, will move through your birth sign. It's a perfect time to study astrology or social sciences. You can do well with electronics and aviation too. New inventions and technologies can make a difference in your life.

March 21 - April 3 Venus in your 4th house makes a square aspect. You will be very generous with loved ones and lavish with purchases for the home. A sense of humor makes all the difference if a social situation is delicate. April's eclipses affect education and travel plans. Check weather conditions and departure times. Inlaws may voice surprising new ideas. New neighbors appear and familiar faces may leave the neighborhood this month. This is especially true near April 17. You are more relaxed concerning money. Saturn leaves your 2nd house of finance early in April after a three-year passage which forced you to economize.

The first three weeks of May Mercury, the Sun, and Mars all highlight home and family matters as they transit your 4th house. Visitors may arrive. It's a good time to plant a garden or initiate a home improvement project. May 20 the Sun and Venus are both in Gemini, your sister air sign. You attract love and affection. A new hobby, game, or love affair adds delight as May closes.

June 1 the Full Moon shines in your 11th house. It's time to decide what you most wish for; set your goals. Friends inform you about fashion trends and world news. June 1-12 Mercury and Mars are in conjunction, forming a volatile square to your Sun. Rise above noise or a tactless remark. Relax and meditate if tensions build. There can be anxiety to release. Faith strengthens you.

June 14-20 promises to be joyful. A soft trine from several Gemini planets in your 5th house allows you to relax and enjoy simple pleasures. A new friend is affectionate and caring. The fine arts brighten leisure hours. Attend a concert, the theater, or an art show. A youthful and whimsical mood surrounds you as you prepare to celebrate Midsummer's Eve.

SUMMER - June 21 to Sept. 22

Get into shape gradually if exercising or doing strenuous physical work June 21-30. The Sun is quincunx Uranus in your birth sign from the 6th house. Health factors in the environment need attention. Pure water and fresh food are essential. Venus stations and turns direct in your 5th house July 1-7. Postpone decisions about love; you may go through a change of heart. Your attitude about clothing styles and recreational or artistic interests is shifting too.

July 8-22 is a wonderful time to toss out debris, to get neat and organized. Minimize stress with efficiency. The last week of July Mercury is in opposition. Other people need time to discuss ideas and views; patience and listening will bring you rewards. A Full Moon in your birth sign July 30 is conjunct retrograde Uranus. This ushers in a sentimental, emotional cycle. Keepsakes and memorabilia remind you of earlier times. Memories are a gift to remind you of how much you've grown.

August brings a solar opposition from the 7th house and a Mercury quincunx. Harmony and balance are a goal in relationships. You will put the security and welfare of others as a top priority. Psychology, law, and social sciences intrigue you.

August 26 - September 11 Mercury hovers on the cusp of your 9th house then turns retrograde. You can complete a partially read book, return to unfinished letters and writing projects. You express ideas eloquently. Sales and promotional skills can be used with ease to facilitate projects you feel are important.

September 12-22 you will feel Mars in Leo bring attention from others. Their expectations and enthusiasms create warmth. Listen to prospects, but don't allow yourself to be overwhelmed and drawn into projects you feel are too difficult or risky. Others are rather forceful.

AUTUMN - Sept. 23 to Dec. 20

There is a sensitivity to subtle energy currents and spiritual entities September 22 - October 8. Mercury is transiting your 8th house. You penetrate secrets and know more about others than they'd ever guess. The eclipse September 26 affects Saturn and your 3rd house. There might be a need to try a different route for daily travel. Reread letters before mailing and be cautious if phone calls drift toward controversy. Use care in what you communicate. On October 10 your ruling planet Uranus completes its retrograde cycle. You will no longer be hampered by deadweight and old issues. A fresh, invigorating quality blows into your life like a fresh autumn breeze.

October 11-26 is perfect for journeys and solving any transportation problems. Mercury is in harmony. You will find TV and radio broadcasts informative and enjoyable. Take time to read seasonal literature in preparation for Hallowmas too. On October 12 there is an eclipse in your 9th house of higher thought which marks a peak in this trend.

October 27 - November 13 ambition burns bright with the Sun and Mercury in your 10th house. You will thrive on a chance to display and test your gifts. Some recognition comes your way.

November 14 - December 4 Mercury joins Pluto to create a sextile from your 11th house. Friendships and group affiliation get you involved in an array of new interests. Politics and humanitarian values are a focus. Those who lack confidence and experience welcome your kind words and courtesy.

December 5-16 avoid sweet, rich foods and late nights. Excesses and indulgences tempt you as Venus completes a square in your 10th house. Postpone holiday shopping. During this time it's easy to spend too much or settle on an item that isn't quite appropriate.

December 17-21 Venus moves forward to pull in favorable aspects from Uranus, Pluto, and Saturn as it enters your 11th house. Accept and issue invitations. Make or buy gifts that suggest humor and a personal message. Your social life is bright and active. You'll be anxious to get to know an acquaintance better. A friendship can propel you toward new spiritual awareness or artistic expression.

WINTER - Dec. 21 to Mar. 20, 1997

A quiet and introspective mood comes in with Yuletide. Your 12th house is very strong with the Sun, retrograde Mercury,

Jupiter, and Neptune there. You can develop inner mental and emotional strength through being sensitive to your own deepest drives. There is an accent on psychology and mental health. Dreams and psychic hunches are plentiful. A bit of service to one who really needs it will be very satisfying December 21 - January 18. The Full Moon in Cancer December 24 lets you know who could use encouragement. On January 3 Mars moves to trine your Sun. A two-month cycle of increased energy and vitality begins.

On January 22 Jupiter, the largest and luckiest planet of all, enters your own birth sign for a year-long passage. By Candlemas its blessings will be felt in the healing of old wounds and opening of opportunities. Jupiter favors an attitude of largesse. Elevate your standards and expectations. This is the start of a whole year of great growth. February 3-26 Venus is in your sign. Love and appreciation surround you. Clothing selected now will be beautiful and serviceable.

February 27 - March 14 physical comfort is important. Fight the cold with warm clothes, plenty of heat, or possibly a vacation in a tropical climate.

March 15-20 Mercury and Saturn conjoin in the 3rd house. You'd enjoy solving a riddle, playing a word game, or learning something new. Alert and alive, your mind relishes a challenge.

PISCES

SPRING - March 21 to June 20

With the coming of spring, brace yourself for a breath of relief and release. Saturn, the celestial heavyweight, is completing a long

75

passage through your sign April 6. Many obstacles and responsibilities are about to dissolve. Finish with old commitments and promises March 20 - April 5. Your energy level is at a peak as Mars is in your birth sign. April's eclipses erupt in your 8th and 2nd houses. New purchases are very important. You'll invest in items which add pleasure and comfort. There can be a deepening awareness of the afterlife and a sense of unity with loved ones who have passed into spirit.

April 18-30 Mercury aspects Neptune, your ruler. Inspired and creative ideas abound. Express yourself through dance, song, or with handicraft projects. Neptune turns retrograde April 29, beginning several months when you will be reflective and can draw on past experiences. Spend May Eve near the waterfront to experience deeper spiritual harmony.

May finds Venus in your 4th house. Your residence is of interest. You could try your hand at interior decorating and entertaining. On May 3 Mars in Taurus will begin a sextile to your Sun which will last until June 13. You can heal and help yourself with positive thought. It's a time when you'll be more self-reliant. Others respond well to advice and suggestions you offer. The New Moon May 17 is conjunct Mercury and Mars; it helps you to focus on definite goals.

June begins with a Full Moon in Sagittarius widely conjunct Pluto in your 10th house. A two-week period follows when you will be emotionally attached to your work. Reform measures will be attractive. Your caring and intensity win admiration. June 14-20 square aspects from Mercury, Mars, Venus, and the Sun show you must get the whole story before making judgments. Keep a sense of humor if people seem a bit abrupt or preoccupied. In love a friendly, casual attitude will make you even more appealing.

SUMMER - June 21 to Sept. 22

Midsummer's Day through June 30 a favorable solar transit softens tension. Younger people are affectionate and ap-

preciative. Try sports and games to brighten leisure hours. July 1-14 Mercury trines you while passing through the 5th house. Creativity is expressed with words. Try adding quips and puns to make a point in conversation. Creative writing efforts can be a spectacular success. A journey is joyful and romantic; don't hesitate if a travel opportunity arises.

July 15-31 Saturn turns retrograde in your 2nd house and applies to squares with Mars and Jupiter. Be conservative with purchases. Old financial obligations and patterns need attention. It isn't the time to consider a risky investment. Postpone selling or giving away possessions you've treasured—you may regret it later.

August finds Mars moving through your sister water sign of Cancer. You will be athletic, strong, and vital. Health improves. A favorable Venus trend starts August 6 and draws new social contacts. A thrilling love affair is possible during August. August 28 brings a Full Moon in Pisces. Others notice you and make suggestions or offer opportunities. Dreams are lucid and vivid. Psychic perceptions are keen. September 1-6 Venus aspects your ruling planet Neptune by opposition. Check to see what commitments others have made for you. There can be a schedule conflict to straighten out. Be cautious about devoting precious time and energy to a lost cause or you could create futile pain for yourself. September 7-22 planets in all three fire signs promise a healthier working environment. You can accomplish a great deal because you are energized by wholesome surroundings.

AUTUMN - Sept. 23 to Dec. 20

Recognize the viewpoints of others. From the equinox through October 8 Mercury will oppose your Sun. There are some conflicting ideas voiced. Be patient, compromise. The eclipse in late September accents your 2nd house. Good or not so good, there is an element of the unpredictable in financial matters. Set aside a little extra money for an unexpected purchase or expense.

October opens with Venus brightening your 7th house. A loved one blossoms with a new beauty or talent. This brings you joy. Legal matters are concluded successfully just before Halloween. Your ruling planet, Neptune, turns direct October 6. This promises a genuine grasp of metaphysical phenomena. October 6-31 is a perfect time to experiment with ghost tracking or a seance. The eclipse on October 12 in your 8th house intensifies this link with the mystical.

November 1-13 the teacher or crusader within you is apparent. You will try to share alternative ideas and knowledge to uplift others. It's a marvelous time for travel. Foreign foods, customs, and music can delight you. The Sun and Mercury aspect you nicely in the 9th house. On November 10 the New Moon in Scorpio illustrates the highest potential of this trend.

November 14-25 a Mercury-Mars aspect in mutable signs creates tense squares and oppositions in your 10th and 7th houses. Keep a good attitude about competition and prepare for some extra projects. It's a very busy cycle. Concentrate with delicate tasks or if using tools or machines. November ends on a happy note with Venus moving into Scorpio the last week of the month. A recipe or gift from another part of the world would be a delightful addition to a holiday gathering. Friends from diverse ethnic or religious backgrounds are charming company November 23 - December 1.

Saturn completes a retrograde cycle in the 2nd house as December opens. You will be able to make a fresh start financially. Look at repeating cycles where money is concerned and draw on wisdom of experience. The first week of December is a good time to search thrift and antique shops for bargains. December 7-21 you will be comforted by a sextile from Capricorn planets in your 11th house. Group travel or spiritual activities are a success. You will cherish friendships and have opportunities to deepen them.

WINTER - Dec. 21 to Mar. 20, 1997

Yule finds you highly visible and creative at work. Venus moves with Pluto through the 10th house until January 9. You will have opportunities to show what you can do with your career. Your manners and appearance can carry you a long way toward realizing a professional aspiration. January 3 a Mars transit which begins in the 8th house heightens analytical skills. You will enjoy deeper insight into the motivations and needs of others for the next eight weeks.

Jupiter enters Aquarius and moves to conjoin Uranus in your 12th house the last week of January. This begins a year-long trend when your subconscious mind will be active. Dreams and visions can intensify. Healing is accelerated by peaceful solitude. You'd benefit from time spent at an ashram or retreat center. Helping abandoned animals or disadvantaged people can be rewarding. The New Moon February 7 is in your 12th house and focuses the parameters of this trend.

On February 27 Venus enters Pisces where it remains through March 20. Winter concludes with a joyful euphoria. New love can warm the cold days. The fine arts provide pleasure, especially dance. The solar eclipse in your own sign March 8 is an ideal time to select personal emblems and insignia. You will give much consideration to image and reputation as winter ends.

Persephone and Pan   Robert Anning Bell, 1894.

And when, in springtime, with sweet-smelling flowers
Of various kinds the earth doth bloom, thou'lt come
From gloomy darkness back— a mighty joy
To gods and mortal man.

                                        —Homeric Hymn

GODDESS of the SPRING

Of all the myths, the concept of the Eternal Return is one of the loveliest. It accounts for a cycle of seasons as dependable as gravity, for an apple never falls up. Summer always follows spring, winter always succeeds autumn, and for this we have Persephone and her mother Demeter to thank, according to the ancients.

In the hurly burly of Greek mythology, awash in crimes of deliciously bizarre nature, the story of Persephone is a notorious tale of kidnapping and ransom.

Demeter is the Earth Mother, provider of the harvest and especially identified with corn, although she has a dark aspect in her underground influence. The death of the growing season and the autumnal sowing of seeds to slumber deep in the earth until awakened in spring defines her powers.

Homer tells us of the famous abduction of Demeter's daughter, sired by the mighty Zeus. While Persephone gathered wild narcissus, she attracted the attention of Hades, King of the Underworld and brother of Zeus. The dark god fell passionately in love with the beautiful maiden at first sight, captured her, and plunged with her in a gold chariot down to the world below.

Demeter heard her daughter's frantic cry for help. "Bitter sorrow seized her heart," says Homer. "Over her shoulders she threw a sombre veil and flew like a bird over land and sea, seeking here, seeking there. For nine days the venerable goddess ranged the world, bearing flaming torches in her hands," the torches symbols of her dark divinity. It was then revealed to her by Hecate that Zeus himself was guilty, decreeing the flower-clad Persephone as his brother's bride.

In a rage, Demeter determined to avoid Olympus and to wander the world until she found her beloved daughter. When the goddess abandoned her duties, its effect was disastrous, for a chill settled on the earth, and nothing grew.

Ignoring the approaching famine, Demeter wandered the earth disguised

as an old woman and sought refuge at Eleusis. Metaneira, who had just been delivered of a son, welcomed the disguised goddess under her roof. Maternal Demeter decided to make the child a god, beyond the reach of illness, old age, and death. She did not feed the boy, but breathed softly on him, anointed him with ambrosia, and at night hid him in the fire like a burning coal to purify what was mortal.

But Metaneira spied the old woman casting the infant into flames and screamed with terror. Incensed, the goddess withdrew the child and appeared in her radiant form. Demeter demanded that a temple be built on the site where initiated mortals would celebrate her mysteries. When the sacred building was prepared, there Demeter remained, still mourning for her lost Persephone.

Despite the wild abduction we cannot report that Hades was a constant husband, for he later dallied with Minthe, a nymph. Persephone, outraged, pursued the unfortunate Minthe and ferociously stamped her into the ground. In sorrow Hades changed the nymph into a plant, the sacred mint, which even today witches stamp on in certain rituals.

High above the subterranean melodrama, Zeus thundered his concern about the perishing of all mankind. He sent gods one by one begging Demeter to return and permit the earth to bear fruits. But Demeter was relentless and at last prevailed. Zeus sent his messenger Hermes to demand the return of Persephone.

Hades complied, but in tricky godlike fashion. Before Persephone left the dark regions, he persuaded her to

eat a pomegranate. And since the jewelbox fruit is the symbol of marriage, Persephone's nibble made the marriage indissoluble.

Stories of divine creatures thrive on complication. Persephone arose to earth in radiance, "a wondrous sight for gods and man." She and her mother embraced, overflowing with joy. But when Demeter questioned her daughter about whether she had eaten anything during her imprisonment, Persephone admitted consuming the fatal pomegranate seeds.

Demeter could not bear to lose her daughter again, yet the garnetlike seeds had forged unbreakable bonds. As a compromise, Zeus decreed that the bride would spend one-third of the year with her husband and two-thirds of the year with her mother.

Demeter agreed and fragrant spring came to warm the hearts and bones of mankind. Buds in their tender green coats sprang out of branches; wheat in its pale beauty emerged from the soil; black bears blinked their way out of caves; flowers spread their sweet rainbows over the earth.

What appears to be merely an exquisite seasonal allegory had a deeper significance, one which found expression in the occult rites celebrated at

Eleusis. "Those mysteries of which no tongue can speak" belong to the height of Greek culture and the most potent site of worship. For centuries scholars have sought in vain to discover the secrets revealed at Eleusis, devoted jointly to Demeter and Persephone.

A few clues have come down to us. We do know that the initiation rites were in two stages, the second following a year's probation. The ceremony began with sacred cakes and goblets of *kykeon*, a drink made of water, barley, and mint. Then the initiates attended a liturgical drama depicting the love union of heaven and earth. But obviously more was presented than the simple mythological commemoration. Scholars conjecture that the ceremony dealt with that deepest of enigmas, death and resurrection. Jung considered the Eleusinian themes a rich source of illumination into the mysticism of the human mind and soul.

Greater Eleusinia, the most important of all Greek observances, took place in the autumn in Athens and Eleusis. The *ephebi*, young men of Athens, proceeded to Eleusis to fetch the *hiera*, sacred objects kept in the temple. The youths returned with great pomp to Athens and placed the *hiera* with all reverence in the Eleusinion at the foot of the Acropolis.

The following day those deemed worthy to participate in the mysteries assembled in Athens at the call of the *hierophant,* high priest. The initiates purified themselves in the sea, along with pigs which they bathed for sacrifice. Finally a solemn procession returned to Eleusis with the *hiera*. And in the vast ritual hall there began one of the most intriguing, most enigmatic, most undivulged rites in religious history.

At the heart of the adoration are both Persephone and Demeter. While the mother figure, like most goddesses, is rich in lore, Persephone is linked with only the one story — but what a marvelous story. She is known by many names. Before her unwilling bridal role the Greeks called her Kore, meaning "virgin," and named her Persephone after the abduction. In utmost reverence the goddess is referred to as "the maiden whose name may not be spoken." Romans adored her as Proserpine. She is often called Queen of the Dead and Goddess of the Spring.

In her aspect as ruler of the underworld, Persephone is frequently identified with Hecate. Both goddesses share dark-of-the-moon and the willow tree as their symbols. Persephone has several other aspects — a sheaf of barley, the bat of dark places, the sweet-smelling narcissus, and of course the pomegranate. But the cock, symbol of rebirth and the new day, tells us most about the cult of Persephone.

—BARBARA STACY

Arthur Rackham

81

THE CELTIC TREE CALENDAR

Beth (Birch)	December 24 to January 20
Luis (Rowan)	January 21 to February 17
Nion (Ash)	February 18 to March 17
Fearn (Alder)	March 18 to April 14
Saille (Willow)	April 15 to May 12
Uath (Hawthorn)	May 13 to June 9
Duir (Oak)	June 10 to July 7
Tinne (Holly)	July 8 to August 4
Coll (Hazel)	August 5 to September 1
Muin (Vine)	September 2 to September 29
Gort (Ivy)	September 30 to October 27
Ngetal (Reed)	October 28 to November 24
Ruis (Elder)	November 25 to December 22

December 23 is not ruled by any tree for it is the "day" of the proverbial "year and day" in the earliest courts of law.

"It takes all the running you can do,
to keep in the same place.
If you want to get somewhere else,
you must run at least twice
as fast as that!"

Apart from the Bible and the works of Shakespeare, the Alice books have probably been quoted more than any other works in the English language. The Red Queen's remark quoted above is one of the most cited passages. From *Through the Looking Glass, and what Alice found there* by Lewis Carroll with illustrations by John Tenniel, 1872.

Talismans

KAMBA, Kenya.

TRIBE UNKNOWN, Nigeria.

AFRICAN MAGIC

The art reproduced here is from a remarkable book: *African Designs from Traditional Sources* by Geoffrey Williams, published by Dover, 31 East 2nd St., Mineola, N.Y. 11501 ($7.95). From 378 illustrations, we've chosen those with magical significance — protective symbols, ceremonial masks, ritual figures and tools. May this offering spark the imagination and creative spirit of those who follow the hidden path.

MASAI *shield*, Kenya.

IBO *water spirit mask*, Nigeria.

SUKU *portal guardian*, Congo.

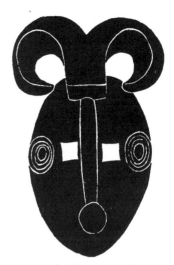

Ogoni society mask
of the YORUBA, Nigeria.

Ritual axe head,
TRIBE UNKNOWN, Dahomey.

FON *altar slab*, Dahomey.   DOGON *cult figure*, Mali.   BEMBE *mask*, Congo.

Life takes on added dimension when you match your activities to the waxing and waning of the Moon. Observe the sequence of her phases to learn the wisdom of constant change within complete certainty.

A New Moon rises with the Sun,
Her waxing half at midday shows,
The Full Moon climbs at sunset hour,
And waning half the midnight knows.

NEW	1997	FULL	NEW	1998	FULL
January 8		January 23	January 28		January 12
February 7		February 22	February 26		February 11
March 8		March 23	March 27		March 12
April 7		April 22	April 26		April 11
May 6		May 22	May 25		May 11
June 5		June 20	June 23		June 9
July 4		July 19	July 23		July 9
August 3		August 18	August 21		August 7
September 1		September 16	September 20		September 6
October 1/31		October 15	October 20		October 5
November 29		November 14	November 18		November 4
December 29		December 13	December 18		December 3

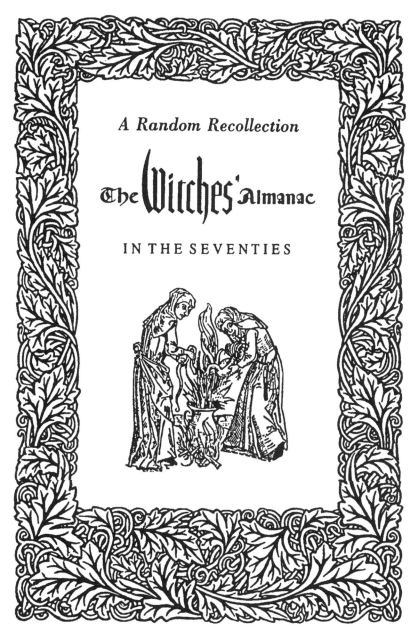

A Random Recollection

ᴛʜᴇ Witches' Almanac

IN THE SEVENTIES

The features we reprint this year are from our 1973/4 edition. The first, *A Case of Mistaken Identity*, corrects an ongoing misunderstanding. A glossary of terms related to witchcraft completes the recollection.

Devil carries off a witch. Olaus Magnus, *Historia de Gentibus Septentrionalibus*, 1555.

A CASE OF MISTAKEN IDENTITY

The doctrine of a link between witchcraft and Satanism surfaced over 400 years ago and persists to the present day. In a climate of ignorance and fear promoted by the mass media, the witch comes under attack in a clear case of mistaken identity. The time has come to address a dangerous situation and correct an unfortunate error.

Followers of witchcraft seldom seek publicity or press for converts. We are content if we can practice our way free of interference. Neither do any of us seek to impose an orthodoxy on others of our persuasion. Within the broad range of this belief system there is room for many paths.

Satanism, however, is essentially alien to our way of thought and over the centuries has caused it much harm. It can do us no good even today.

To explain why this is so I must discuss witchcraft in a flat, objective way. This may seem out of place, for to those who can know it at all the craft is revealed in direct mystical experiences. Our own perceptions are the touchstone by which we judge its truth. If what I say about it

doesn't jibe with your experience there is no way I can convince you or prove you wrong.

Nevertheless witchcraft exists in history. It embodies an extremely ancient tradition that was known in one form or another over much of the world. If it represents a survival of druidism or a cult of the horned god, as some scholars have said, it also was known in the mysteries of ancient Greece, the following of the Moon goddess, and many other forms.

The arrival of Christianity, often imposed by the sword and the rack, all but extinguished the old ways. But they survived in historical accounts that can be interpreted by stripping away the bias, and more importantly they survived through cleverly disguised folklore and secret practice in remote areas where the church's control was weak. It is this survival that permits us to feel connected with the ancient tradition now that the power of Christianity is fading.

Satanism, on the other hand, springs from Christianity itself and its sources in the Near East. If one reads the Bible as a series of documents produced over time rather than as eternally true divine revelation, one can see that the nature of Satan underwent an evolution in ancient Palestine just as that of Jahveh (Jehovah) did.

At first Jahveh was one of many gods of different tribes and holy places. He rewarded the worship and sacrifices of the Israelites with prosperity and victory in battle and hence earned their allegiance. He cared little for other peoples. Satan then was another god not much different from Jahveh, perhaps derived from the Baal of other Canaanite tribes. In the book of Job, for instance, Satan appears as an antagonist of Jahveh in a rather friendly contest not unlike chess except that it involves a mortal man and his family.

Later, however, the Satan who tempts Jesus in the wilderness is clearly the embodiment of evil. This concept of an evil force opposed to a wholly good God came from the Zoroastrian religion to the east and is plainly expressed in the Essene writings recovered in the so-called Dead Sea scrolls.

As formulated in Manichaeism, this doctrine was denounced as heresy by the fathers of the early church. They opted instead for the doctrine of an all-powerful God. This choice meant, however, that God must be responsible for evil as well as good. Since then the church fathers have had to explain evil as something necessary for the ultimate working out of God's inscrutable plan for the world, which can be only good. This position has not been an easy one to defend through ages of war,

pestilence, and famine, and a strain of Manichaeism has persisted even among the most devout Christians.

Worship of Satan, who, independent of God's will or not, remained in the Scriptures, arose in the Middle Ages as a reaction against Christianity. In its purest form it simply reversed everything Christian. Anything the church defined as good was evil and vice versa. The ceremonies were a turning upside down of the mass and the other sacraments. As such Satanism clearly had nothing to do with true witchcraft.

The two practices were confused originally not by followers of either one but by the church, which regarded anything not Christian as devilish. The unspeakable tortures of the witch hunts produced confessions that confirmed this view. Sensation-seeking Satanists abetted the confusion when it served to their advantage. Further confusion arose from essentially literary traditions like the Faust story, in which occult powers were conferred in return for future consignment of the soul to the Christian (but only loosely Biblical) hell. Only the advent of an age that can examine church dogma rationally from without has made it possible to separate these strands of un-Christian practice from the anti-Christian.

Satanism, then, can be the worship of an ancient Near Eastern god; or it can invoke the name of Satan for unhistorical purposes, such as glorifying man's animal nature. In either form it may be unobjectional but it is unrelated to witchcraft. Or it can be a worship of the evil principle through a conscious inversion of Christian ritual. As such it is not only silly but dangerous.

Why silly? Because evil is not something that can have an authentic, independent existence. Gods are revealed through the experience of a people with their physical and spiritual surroundings. Evil is not a god in this sense. Rather it is an idea — that is, a quality we attribute to things, not something inherent in things.

Evil is not a trait of an object, like a color, that we can perceive through our senses. It is not a disease that infects us like bacteria, nor is it the gap that appears when a person falls short of meeting some concept of human nature (for who can say what human nature really is?) Nothing is evil in itself; the evil comes from our judging it so.

Of course there can be a general consensus that some action is evil. Most of us would say this of wanton murder, for example. But there can be cases where some of us would say a killing was wanton and others would say it was justified. There can be cases where unlike a few centuries ago, a killing is considered not wanton because the killer was insane and not responsible for his actions. In the final analysis, evil is a matter of definition that can change with time, place and people.

The supernatural agencies invoked in true witchcraft are neither good nor evil. They may aid us or harm us or ignore us, but we can call these actions good and evil only in terms of their effects on us. To someone else they may look quite the opposite. The most a witch can honestly say is that he or she believes these agencies are there. Witchcraft really is the search to discover their nature and put oneself in harmony with them. Nothing can be further from this spirit than Satanism, and it would behoove us to do everything we can to oppose such nonsense.

—CHARLES E. PEPPER
1931 - 1976

GLOSSARY

ADEPT — A skilled practitioner of the occult arts.

ALCHEMY — Medieval science dedicated to turning base metals into gold.

AMULET — A charm worn to avert evil and attract good luck.

ARADIA — The legendary daughter of deities Diana and Lucifer destined to teach witchcraft to mortals.

ARCANE — Secret knowledge.

ARCHETYPE — The original model or pattern.

ASTRAL BODY — Spirit body.

ATAVISM —Of or pertaining to a remote ancestor in instinctive memory.

ATHAME — Black-hilted knife used in the rites of a ceremonial magician.

AUGURY — Divination.

AURA — A halo, or emanation of light surrounding an individual.

AVALON — The Celtic abode of the blessed; paradise of Arthurian legend.

BALEFIRE — A great fire blazing in the open air; a bonfire.

BANE — That which destroys life.

BANSHEE—Gaelic spirit whose wail warns of approaching death.

BARD—Celtic poet; a singer of tales.

BELTANE — Celtic name for the festival celebrated on May Eve.

BLOCULA — An Elfdale county estate where Swedish witches attended the sabbat festivals.

BLOODSTONE — A green gem sprinkled with red spots; the heliotrope of magic.

BOOK OF SHADOWS — A collection of ancient rituals, chants, spells and enchantments copied down in the handwriting of a witch.

BRIDE — Brigit, Bridget, or Brid is the pre-Celtic goddess of Ireland symbolizing the promise of spring.

BROCKEN—The highest peak in the Hartz mountains of Northern Germany known as a gathering place for witches.

BY KYNDE — By nature, or instinct.

CABALA — Hebraic system of mystical thought; an esoteric doctrine of urban medieval society.

CAIRN — A Gaelic term for a stone pile accumulating when clearing a field for planting.

CANDLEMAS — A festival of light celebrated on the eve of February 2 — Feast of Bride.

CHALICE — A silver cup used in sacred ceremonies of witchcraft.

CHANGELING — A child secretly exchanged for another in infancy.

CONE OF POWER — The collected force of powerful wills focused on a single purpose.

COVEN—A congregation of witches.

CULT—A shared system of belief or worship.

CUNNING MAN — Known in Elizabethan England as one thought able to combat the will of witches.

DEASIL—To move sunwise or clockwise, from left to right. A charm performed by going three times around an object carrying fire in the right hand.

DEJA VU — Fleeting personal memory of a previous life.

DEMETER — Greek goddess of the earth; known to the Romans as Ceres.

DIANA — Roman goddess of the Moon and the hunt; called Artemis by the Greeks.

DIONYSIAN MYSTERIES — Rites of worship celebrated to honor the god of the vine and earth.

DIRAE — Omen.

DRUID — One of the priestly class of Celtic culture. A modern follower of ancient ways.

DUALISM — A philosophical concept of opposing principles which form the ultimate nature of the universe as, for example, good and evil.

DYAD — Two units; a pair.

ELEUSINIAN MYSTERIES — Rites dedicated to the worship of Demeter and Persephone.

EQUINOX — The time when day and night are of equal length.

ESBAT — Weekly meeting of witches.

EVIL EYE — A baleful glance capable of causing harm.

EXORCISM — A Christian ritual practiced to expel evil spirits.

FAMILIAR — Animal helper of a witch in casting enchantments and working spells.

FETCH — Apparition.

FOX FIRE — A mysterious light hovering over marshy ground at night; the *ignis fatuus* or will-o-the-wisp.

FREYA — Nordic goddess of love for whom Friday is named.

GNOSTICISM — The system of thought, philosophy, and religion which holds mankind may possess inner knowledge by direct revelation.

GRIMOIRE — A text of magical rites and spells.

HALLOWMAS — November Eve festival of witchcraft.

HECATE — Patroness of witchcraft; a triple goddess of the Moon, earth, and underworld.

HERODIAS — Goddess of witches; Diana as Queen of the Night.

HEX — A spell or a charm derived from the German word for witchcraft.

HIEROPHANT — High priest of the Eleusinian mysteries.

HUBRIS — Man's exasperation with fate and life's limitations.

I CHING — Chinese Book of Changes; collected wisdom used for divination.

INCANTATION — Chant spoken slowly with firm intent.

JANUS — Roman solar god who watched both the rising and setting suns.

LA TENE — The Iron Age in Europe dating from 500 B.C. to A.D. 100.

LAMMAS — Festival of witchcraft held on August eve to insure good harvest.

LIGATURE — A binding.

LOKI — Nordic god of fire.

LUGHNASSAD — Celtic name for the August Eve celebration.

MACROCOSM / MICROCOSM — The universe as contrasted to man. What is equal above, is equal below.

MAGUS — Wise man.

NEED-FIRE — A flame produced by friction in ceremony used to ignite the bonfires of May Eve.

ODIN — Nordic god of wisdom and poetry.

OIMELC — Celtic name for the celebration held on the eve of February 2.

OVERLOOK — To cast a glance of power for good or ill.

OWL TIME — Between midnight and one o'clock; the 13th hour.

PENTACLE — Five-pointed star, an ancient symbol of perfection used from the time of Pythagoras, Greek philosopher and mathematician, 6th century B.C.

PERSEPHONE — The daughter of Demeter / Ceres who was abducted by the god of the underworld. Her return each year symbolizes springtime and rebirth.

PHILTRE — A potion prepared to produce a magical effect, especially a love charm.

PSYCHE — The human soul; the mind; the inner thought.

RITES OF PASSAGE — Human transitions celebrated at birth, puberty, marriage and death.

ROODMAS — Anglo-Saxon name for the May Eve festival.

RUNES — Germanic alphabet derived in large measure from the Greek and Roman and formed with straight lines to facilitate carving on stone and wood.

SABBAT — Feast. Major sabbats are November Eve, February 1, May Eve, and August Eve. The lesser sabbats are celebrated at winter and summer solstices; spring (vernal) and autumnal equinoxes.

SAMHAIN — The Celtic name for the November Eve celebration; Hallowmas.

SATANISM — Christian devil worship; an inversion or parody of Christian faith.

SCRY — To divine by means of crystal ball, mirror or other reflective surface.

SHAMAN — Sorcerer of primitive tribes. A medium between the visible and the spirit world.

SIGNATURES, DOCTRINE OF — The belief that each plant bears a visible key to its use.

SOLITARY — One who practices the art of witchcraft alone.

SOLSTICE — The longest day of the year, Midsummer Day, June 21; the shortest day, December 21, when the Sun begins its return and the days lengthen.

SOOTH — Truth.

SWAN-ROAD — The sea.

TALISMAN — An object marked under certain conditions of the heavens to act as a charm against evil.

TRADITIONALS — A term used to designate members of the witch-cult who practice rites handed down through the generations; hereditary witches.

VATES — Prophets.

WALPURGISNACHT — Germanic name for the May Eve festival.

WATCHERS — The sleepless ones or "fallen angels" of Hebrew legend who mated with the daughters of men to whom they taught the forbidden arts.

WARLOCK — An Anglo-Saxon term of derision, i.e., a liar and betrayer of trust.

WIDDERSHINS — Backward, or in a direction contrary to the apparent motion of the Sun. To move counterclockwise.

WITCH — From the Anglo-Saxon "wiccan" or wise. One blessed with supernatural gifts.

WITCH BALLS — Spheres of colored glass intended to thwart evil spirits and protect the home.

WORT — Any plant or herb.

WYRD — Anglo-Saxon goddess of destiny.

YULE — Norse feast celebrating winter solstice.

ZOROASTER — Prophet who flourished in Persia about 1000 B.C.

FULL MOON NAMES

The tradition of naming the year's Full Moons began during the early centuries of the Christian era in rural England. A few reflect the influence of the Roman occupation, but the majority relate to farm activity.

Aries — SEED. Sowing season and symbol of the start of the new year.

Taurus — HARE. The sacred animal was associated in Roman legends with springtime and fertility.

Gemini — DYAD. The Latin word for a pair refers to the twin stars of the constellation Castor and Pollux.

Cancer — MEAD. During late June and most of July the meadows, or meads, were mowed for hay.

Leo — WORT. When the sun was in Leo the worts (from the Anglo-Saxon wyrt - plant) were gathered to be dried and stored.

Virgo — BARLEY. Persephone, virgin goddess of rebirth, carries a sheaf of barley as symbol of the harvest.

Libra — BLOOD. Marking the season when domestic animals were sacrificed for winter provisions.

Scorpio — SNOW. Scorpio heralds the dark season when the Sun is at its lowest and the first snow flies.

Sagittarius — OAK. The sacred tree of the Druids and the Roman god Jupiter is most noble as it withstands winter's blasts.

Capricorn — WOLF. The fearsome nocturnal animal represents the "night" of the year. Wolves were rarely seen in England after the 12th century.

Aquarius — STORM. A storm is said to rage most fiercely just before it ends, and the year usually follows suit.

Pisces — CHASTE. The antiquated word for pure reflects the custom of greeting the new year with a clear soul.

Libra's Full Moon occasionally became the WINE moon when a grape harvest was expected to produce a superior vintage.

TO: The Witches' Almanac, P.O. Box 4067, Middletown, RI, 02842

Name _____

Address _____

City _____ State _____ Zip _____

WITCHCRAFT being by nature one of the secretive arts it may not be as easy to find us next year. If you'd like to make sure we know where *you* are why don't you send us your name & address? You'll certainly hear from us.

Publication Date: May 1996

Wisdom Through the Seasons

Edited by Elizabeth Pepper and John Wilcock

A Treasury of wisdom from Aristotle to W.C. Fields.
from Capra Press / 240 pp. / 6 x 9" / $15.95

Order Form

Each edition of *The Witches' Almanac* is a unique journey through the classic stylings of Elizabeth Pepper and John Wilcock. Limited numbers of previous years' editions are available.

LIVE BY THE MOON and know the magic of true love. This is the theme of ElizabethPepper's LOVE CHARMS. It's a treasury of love charms to use now and ever after.

Pages culled from the original (no longer available) issues of *The Witches'Almanac* published annually throughout the 1970's are offered in two tasteful booklets: A RANDOM RECOLLECTION #1, the revised edition; and A RANDOM RECOLLECTION #2. For those who missed us the first time around; keepsakes for those who remember.

1996 - 1997 The Witches' Almanac _____ @ $6.95 + $2.50 postage _____

1995 - 1996 The Witches' Almanac _____ @ $6.95 + $2.50 postage _____

1994 - 1995 The Witches' Almanac _____ @ $5.95 + $2.50 postage _____

1993 - 1994 The Witches' Almanac _____ @ $5.95 + $2.50 postage _____

Love Charms _____ @ $5.95 + $2.50 postage _____

Random Recollection #1 _____ @ $3.95 + $1.50 postage _____

Random Recollection #2 _____ @ $3.95 + $1.50 postage _____

Send check or money order payable to The Witches' Almanac Mail Order Dept., PO Box 4067, Middletown, RI, 02842.

SUBTOTAL _____

TOTAL _____